WHAT I BELIEVE

WHAT I BELIEVE

A Book about Teaching, Training Horses, and the Brain

CARL BISSONETTE

CONTENTS

Chapter 1: Where It All Started

WHERE IT ALL STARTED

If you can imagine this scene, it would pull at all your heartstrings. In a little three-bedroom house with brown calico carpet, the 90's country music blaring on the television, there in the room was a young boy with red hair. He was wearing nothing but cowboy boots that came most of the way up his short little legs. On top of his head, he was wearing his dad's old brown cowboy hat. The boy knew he was not supposed to mess with his dad's hat, but he could not resist the opportunity to play cowboy. Sitting on top of a rocking horse, visions of wrangling up cattle, sitting by a campfire, and riding a horse in the sweet sagebrush were all this young boy could dream about. I cannot place my finger on that moment when that burning desire to be a cowboy was placed on my heart, but as long as I can remember, being a cowboy is all I wanted to be. That desire has been with me for as long as I can remember.

I grew up in Port Angeles, Washington. I felt the old cowboy songs I listened to might be the closest I would ever get to living the cowboy dream.

Relentless would be an understatement to describe my character. Every Christmas, birthday, and any other holiday a young boy could wish and dream about a present, I would always ask for a horse. The problem I faced was that I was a cowboy growing up in a small suburban town. Very rarely would I ever see a cowboy hat. Port Angeles, you were likelier to see a logger in his corks than a punchy cowboy with his flat brim and tall top boots.

Besides logging, this town had a mill, a hospital, and fishing. None of this excited the cowboy that was bred into my soul. My mom jokes that I came out of the womb with cowboy boots on my feet. I was the odd sheep in the herd of cows. No one could understand where this desire to be a cowboy came from, but you could not deny that it was there. When you ask first graders what they want to become, the dreams of doctors, lawyers, police officers, professional baseball player, and fireman tends to exist for a short time. That was not the case with me.

In my first year of pre-school, I know this statement must have caught some people's attention. I was riding my bike to my friend's house, and I was hit by a truck. Another neighbor found me twenty feet in the bramble. I ended up breaking my femur. With me being as young as I was, they did not want to put a rod in my leg, so I was left to heal naturally. Unfortunately, the muscle was pulling the bone past where the bones needed to be. I had to be put in traction. They had to lift my broken leg a foot and a half to get it into the sling. At that time, I can say that was the worst pain I have ever experienced.

Each day, the doctor or nurse would come by and place another weight onto the other end of the sling. The weight pulled my leg apart until the two broken bones lined up with each other. The first cast I had went down both legs. They had to turn me sideways to get me through most normal-sized doors. My dad built a costume wheelchair out of a jogging cart and a piece of plywood so my parents could take me out of the house. My second cast went around the hip and down the broken leg. This new cast allowed me a little more mobility. Because of this, my parents felt it best to hold me back in pre-school for another year.

To follow, I would end up having an asthma attack. I remember we had family photos, and it became harder and harder to smile as the minutes ticked on. By the end of the day, you could see in the pictures that I was very sick. My parents gave me medicine when we got home, and I could not keep it down. Not being able to get the medicine in my system, worried my parents enough to take me to the hospital. Thank the lord that they did. I completely stopped breathing in the parking lot of the hospital. I remember the nurse saying, "You better start crying now because it will hurt." My dad lost count of the number of shots they threw in me, to try and get me going again. The next thing I remember, I was waking up in an oxygen hood. What was funny about this time in hospital was what the nurse walked into. I had a rabbit hide that was like my blankie. Grandma brought it to me to give me a little comfort in the hospital. The oxygen hood caused all the hair to stick to my face. The nurse came into my room quite surprised, as she saw a kid with a hairy face, until she figured out the cause of my condition.

So, all of that led me to believe that I was a bit of a miracle and that God must want me on this earth for a bit longer. The blessing in starting life in this manner is you appreciate each day that you are alive. I also grew up knowing that no moment is guaranteed to you. Growing up with this blessing led me to become a person that doesn't waste my time daydreaming. If you dream about doing it today and don't do it, then you may die tomorrow without at least giving it a shot. I approached most things in this manner. If you are going to do something, you should do it to the best of your ability. I would say this influenced me to have some perfectionist traits. That being said, I do have some things in my life that are just for the simple pleasure of doing it with no desire to be great at it. For me, this was music. I play guitar, play the violin, play the cello, play the harmonica, sing and other instruments. I just loved being around music, and I was content with it at whatever level I was playing.

In school, I remember a vivid disdain repulse to learning about Native American studies. I have gained an appreciation for learning about native studies. But as a kid, I wanted to know more about cowboys. So, learning about anything other than cowboys was repulsive. In the third grade, my teacher thought I might have a learning disorder because I was not reading at the same level as my classmates. Luckily, I have a very wise Grandma. When she heard this news, she bought me a cowboy book. Turns out, I had no problem reading. I was just stubborn. I didn't want to read about cartoon characters that were unreal. I wanted to read about cowboys, horses, ranching, and the range.

Growing up in a reservation town shaped me in many ways. I joke now that the kids did not like me because I was white, also since I was a redhead, and they did not care for me because I was a cowboy. Those lessons were taught to me by those mean kids, I will never forget. They helped shape my understanding of horses, my students, and others. Though I was almost a year older than my classmates, I was the weak, skinny kid till my junior year in high school. When I started high school in my Junior year, I was lucky if I weighed 100 pounds soaking wet.

Middle school is when I started riding consistently. Before that, my mom's hair lady was kind enough to let me borrow one of their horses. That is when I got to start practicing the skills I would need for rodeo. I rode with the gal's two kids. We all became pretty good friends. There was a younger brother, but he was not interested in the horses at all.

Then, while practicing, I got an offer from an older gentleman to ride his horses. Getting to ride his horses worked out better because I could ride the bus up to his place. I would clean stalls, feed, fix fences, trim the horse's feet, buck hay, and ride. Working for him is where my horse spirit came alive. My mom knew nothing about horses. My mom would take me to the rodeos, but she never had any input other than telling me the good job I did or better luck next time. I had a ton of time to figure it out on my own. Looking back, this is where I probably developed my if it works philosophy, then use it; if it doesn't work, then don't use it. The idea of wanting to be a fine horseman never really crossed my mind. It was more about getting the horse to do the things I would need it to do to be competitive in rodeo. At that time, I competed in all the events but bareback riding. I continued all the rodeo events into college when people would ask, "Why didn't I ride bareback horses?" I would chuckle and say, "Because it scares me." It was true, too! Bulls and saddle bronc never really scared me, but bareback riding did! Some of the worst wrecks I have seen in rodeo have been in bareback riding. When you let go, your hand does not always come out of the tightly fitted riggen.

During that middle school time, I also started shoeing horses. The guy who taught me would turn into a friend and, even more so, a parent figure to me. Sometimes, I was not tough enough to do something because of my small stature, but he never let me use that as an excuse. It was always more like finding another way to do it. He had two kids of his own. Between watching the kids, shoeing horses, roping, and farming, I spent much of my time with his family. I would also buck hay for his father during the summers. Everything I did was to be more self-sufficient with horses. Growing up, we didn't have much money. So, I worked most of my trades off. If I needed my horse shod, my buddy would help me because I worked for him. When I needed hay for my horse, the guy would give it to me because I bucked hay for him for the summer. Slowly but surely, I was putting all the pieces together.

My older brother was into more traditional sports. In high school, he mainly focused on soccer and basketball. He was a great athlete. Both my brother and I played on select traveling soccer and basketball teams. We frequently went in different directions each week- end. Subsequently, my mom tended to take me, and my dad took my brother. When I got big into rodeo, I soon only focused on that. So, instead of traveling to soccer and basketball games, that got replaced by traveling to rodeos.

I did not enjoy the schooling process. Many parts of it did not make sense to me. My childhood struggles have trickled into my current belief on how a teacher can support a classroom. I was the typical kid in that my favorite subjects would be lunch, PE, recess, and when school got out for summer. I did have some good memories of some good teachers. At that time, I believed most of my teachers did not teach well. I still hold this idea to be true. The following paragraphs will discuss some memorable stories I have from school.

When I was young, we went on a family trip to Disneyland. Getting to get to go on this trip was exciting. Flying to Disneyland may have been my first time flying. When we got there, it had all the magical lure that a kid could ask for. My two favorite places in the park were the canoe ride and Huck Island. There was a gift shop on Huck Island, and my mom bought me the most incredible fake rubber knife. It looked just like a bowie knife but was black and rubber. I loved it. As a young kid, I had plans to be a trapper and a cowboy, so that knife would help me skin all them pretend coyotes. Several months after I was home from the trip, I must have used my school backpack to pack up some of my coolest toys to hang out with a friend. Somehow, I had forgotten that the rubber knife was still in my backpack. While in line waiting to go into class, as I was rummaging for my school supplies, I found that rubber knife. It was an honest mistake. I meant no harm by it, but it was in my backpack at school. I told my best friend and asked him what I should do. Instead of giving me sound advice, he told the teacher I had a rubber knife. I got into trouble, and she held onto it until she could give it to my mother. Luckily, my mom understood my innocence, and she wasn't mad. It pained me that I accidentally did something wrong that got me into trouble.

The following story happened in middle school. I re-tell this story quite a bit. I was playing in the school orchestra. I played the cello. By then, I had guitar lessons since I was eight and played the violin for one school year. The teacher we had for fourth, fifth, and middle school was a true professional musician. It was told to me by my brother that he was a site reader for Disney. Being able to sight read meant they would give him a piece of sheet music, and he would then have thirty minutes to prepare with the other orchestra members. Then, they expected him to play the sheet of music without flaw. They had so little time to practice; it was their way of ensuring that the musicians would not be able to steal the music.

I digress; I was in my second or third year of middle school. I was not too fond of the practice charts we had to fill out. While playing the cello, I could not bring the cello on the bus, so I could not practice. Since I was not practicing, it was hurting my grade. I talked to the teacher. I explained to him that I wanted to become something other than great at music, but I did enjoy being around music. I explained that I only wanted to practice during class. If I was hindering the progression of the orchestra and he needed me to sit out for a bit, I would gladly oblige him. I also told him if he didn't think I was good enough for the concerts that, I wouldn't show up. Or, I would fake play so as not to raise suspicion with the other students. I didn't want them to think that he was treating me differently. I would do all of these things if he would stop hurting my grade because of the practice charts. Surprisingly, he agreed. Although he never asked me to sit out of practice or a concert, I received a B grade. I was happy with that compromise. This story has dramatically shaped my philosophy on teaching pedagogy.

Another time, it was my sophomore English class. I had a great teacher who understood me. Previously, I had struggled with English. Since there was not an English rule book, it was an inferior study. It was subject to one's opinion, making it subjective instead of objective. So, if the teacher didn't like you, you were screwed, or at least that was my thought. My struggle had parts and pieces that, at the time, I did not understand.

As a kid, I had to get tubes put into my ears. They figured I was lip-reading about 85% of the time. If I did not hear the words correctly, I struggled to spell them correctly. Also, I was starting to hang around the rodeo crew. Since everyone travels so much, the rodeo language starts blending to create its beautiful nuances. The slurs to my speech didn't help me out in English class none much either. If you have been around rodeo people much, that last sentence will make perfect sense. But if you are an English teacher, your eyes and ears are probably bleeding. To me, English class was just a bunch of rules, and when I read books, the few I was reading, I would see others breaking the rules I was learning. It was hypocritical of the teachers to have us read books with the mistakes that we could not make in our writing. I struggle to relate to anything hypocritical. At times, my family would say I was honest to a fault.

Anyway, I had not been doing well with my essays because of my grammar and spelling. Luckily, I had the brass about myself to self-advocate. At the time, I did not know what self-advocate meant, but I already knew that I needed a different education than my peers. We had a 500-word or more essay that we needed to write explaining who we were as a person. I asked the teacher if he would waive the grammar and spelling if I rhymed the whole essay. Surprisingly, he agreed to it. That was the first English paper I got an A on in high school. In a lot of ways, I made it harder on myself. I knew I was good at the creative side of writing. Having a teacher willing to work with me instead of dictating to me earned my trust and respect. I was learning how to get the education I wanted and desired from the academic system.

Another thing that made me unique happened in my last year of college. My brother got married, and I got kicked out of his house. Some details may differ from my view of what happened, but if he wants his side of the story, he is welcome to write his book and explain things his way. We both had bought five acres next to each other. He had a house built, and I built a barn. You can tell the difference in our priorities. I lived with him for a year. Somewhere in the middle of that year, he started to date his now wife. They were engaged that winter and were planning to marry in June. As we were leading up to the summer, we sat down and talked about what the summer might look like. They did not want me to live in the house during the summer because they needed their honeymoon time together. I explained that since I worked for the Christian horse camp, I was gone from Sunday till Friday, and they could have their honeymoon time then. I would only be there for two nights. They informed me it would not be good enough for them, so I moved out at the end of June. I was officially homeless. It didn't bother me because I had a bed roll to live out of. Some weekends, I was gone judging junior rodeos, so I was camping at the fairgrounds. The other weekends, my dad and I built a two-hundred-square-foot cabin with a loft in it. My brother did help me some with the construction. By the start of the next school year, I had a place to live.

In my little cabin, I had a sink with a two-gallon hot water tank, a mini fridge, a microwave, a little convection oven, and a hot plate. I had a couch down below and a rocking chair for the company who might come over. There was a ladder that I could put up that went into the loft. I had my bed up in my loft. Outside, I had a porta-potty. I had to go to my grandma's house to shower, and I would do that every other day. She admittedly did my laundry for me to help me out. I lived in that cabin for four years. Three of the years were during my professional career. It was a tiny home before tiny homes were a thing. It taught me many great things I still hold onto today. I had to keep things organized. I had to decide what was important to me. I had to become confident in myself.

One month into living in the cabin, my computer sound went out, so I could no longer watch movies. I went for two months with just a radio. I was slowly going crazy. I would have some deep thoughts of the isolation. I felt myself fading out of society. There were times when I felt like people did not care about me. That is a tough place to be. I ended up buying a little television and a DVD player. Just seeing humans and hearing them speak did wonders to dull the feeling of isolation. There were still some tough times I would go through, but it made me tougher for it. After four years of living in the cabin, that time helped me to build the equity in the property. The equity allowed me to get a new loan to build a house.

When I moved into the house the first night, I had to go to the bathroom. So, I got up and went outside. I was looking up at the stars and realized that I had three bathrooms inside. It was a surreal experience that one can only acquire after four years of a routine of going outside. During the summer, the porta-potty would about melt you. The worst was during the winter, though. I rigged up a little space heater, and it was alright if you turned it on ten minutes before you had to go. Sometimes, things would hit, and you didn't have time to warm up the porta-potty. Some of those winters got cold, like negative degrees cold. Come to find out that is cold enough to freeze the porta-potty water. That frozen water made for a lousy updraft.

Hopefully, these stories will lay the foundation to help you understand the journey you are about to take. Intertwined in these following chapters will be the parts and pieces that will slowly come together to create the big picture of what has shaped my philosophy with teaching students, training horses, and what we need to know about the brain to develop effective change of behavior. In trying to explain it, my mind is painting a picture of bread-making. Salt, sugar, flour, yeast, and water are no more related to each other than training horses, teaching, and the brain, but when you put it all together, it has created my understanding of pedagogy. This pedagogy has helped me to be successful in the multiple disciplines that I am in. Understand, my idea of being successful has less to do with me and more with the other side of the equation, helping the students, horses, and other teachers. In creating the right atmosphere, many things can thrive. In the wrong atmosphere, the same seed may become no different than a grain of sand. I am writing this in hopes that through my journey, if this can help you somehow, I am doing my due diligence to provide you with this sustenance.

Chapter 2: Learning To Train Horses

LEARNING TO TRAIN HORSES

Now, onto the fun stuff! I was 16, and I had been training horses for people for about a year. What I accomplished then training horses came from my ability to reason and problem solve. At that point in life, I had not become a great trainer, but people could see I could read a horse. I often compare it to a Border Collie pup. The dog has the breeding to work stock; it wants to work stock, and as a pup, it will work stock better than a lab. With training, it can become truly great at working stock.

There was a buzz about this new guy in town training horses. I was skeptical. The first time I watched him work a horse, I thought that he trained on the horse a bit hard, but at the time, I didn't fully understand what he was doing. I could see he had control of the horse. Honestly, I could recognize that he could control a horse in ways that I couldn't. I didn't need those things to train a rodeo horse, or so I thought.

I was training horses for a guy out of Canada. He had some nice horses. I was teaching one of the horses to become a calf roping horse. He showed potential and was a quick learner. I thought to myself, If I could teach my calf roping horses to slide two more feet in the stop, that would help keep more calves standing. Keeping calves on their feet is ideal in calf roping because it allows you to be faster on the ground. Somehow, the guy I was training for had ties to the guy who was also training around town that I had heard about.

I had another friend going to one of his weekend clinics, and she invited me along. That is when I saw what he had to offer. I explain to people my view of the level of hierarchy of greatness. You can be good at something, great at something, professional at something, or artistic. Artist in their trade is the highest level of performance. They can talk all the talk of a professional, but an artist will create something new that will change the profession for generations. Max was an artist when it came to training horses. After the clinic, I had the opportunity to chat with Max. He was a kind gentleman who loved the ladies. I explained to him how I wanted to get the couple extra two-foot sliding stops on my calf roping horses. I also explained that I had no intention of going into reining. I just wanted to learn these skills to help my rodeo horses. I told him, "If I have to lay down while you piss on me to make my horses stop like yours, I would be okay with that." He chuckled and agreed to take me on. He said, "When you make me money, I will pay you."

I could write an entire book on what he taught me about horses. I would go up the mountain daily in my rickety old truck to ride and learn. It did not take long, and he taught me how to start colts his way.

He had a fantastic mix between the old school and the new school way of training. He had ridden rough pens in British Columbia, so he knew how to get on one and ride the buck out of it, but he also learned how to start a colt in a way that most of them never buck. Later in his years, he developed the philosophy that it is much easier on the body if you start a colt in a manner where it never bucks. You can be the best trainer in the world, but if you have a broken leg, a broken back, or some other injury, it does not matter how good of a trainer you are. You can also be the best bronc rider in the world, but every time a colt goes to bucking, you increase your chances of getting hurt. Even if you do everything correctly, youngsters can trip and fall while they are bucking. As a trainer, you cannot be afraid of pain, but you must do what you can to keep yourself in the training world as long as possible.

It did not take long, and Max soon paid me to start colts. We became best friends. We could both talk about horses for hours. Each time we would have these talks, we were both learning more in the process. The top professionals will agree every horse teaches you something more about training horses. If you are willing to listen to the horse, it will show you what they need. It did not take long, and all I was thinking about was horses. I found I understand horses better than I know people. I joke at least a horse is honest about what they are feeling. During that time, I was also having a hard time at school. I did not fit in. With horses, they didn't care how cool I was.

I believe some people are born with horse blood in their veins, and I am one of those people. God gave me a special gift to read and understand horses. When you have this gift from God, horses can see it too. Close to 99% of the time, I can get on someone else's horse and be riding it better than they can by the end of a training session. I say these things not to brag about myself but to give credit to God and Max. God gave me the breeding, and Max trained me into a horseman. I was becoming like the border collie that worked cattle well and listened well.

My life at the time was a constant hustle. Most of the time I would have at least three jobs. I was riding for Max, working at the tank yard (pouring pre-cast concrete into septic and water tanks), shoeing horses, and training horses on my own. Those were the main jobs I worked, but I had many more that I accumulated throughout my high school years.

It did not take long, and I trained horses better than most owners could ride. So, that natural progression led me to teach people how to ride their horses. If you walked into the scene, it would make you turn your head sideways. You could often catch me on a horse or standing in an arena explaining to adults twice my age, who had been riding horses for longer than I was alive, how to pick up a feel. I would be showing them how to set their body up to allow the horse to be able to do a maneuver. Or I would explain why what they were doing didn't make sense to the horse or how they could communicate their cue in a better way.

I could train horses and teach people for hours. I never got tired of helping the owners and the horses. I loved it. The best part about it was people would pay me money to get to do what I loved doing. In addition, each person I trained for allowed me to learn more about horses each time. I was building a program and learning tons along the way.

It all made good sense to me. Horses are herd animals. They find comfort in the herd. There is usually a dominant male and a dominant female in every band of horses. From there, all the other horses sort their order out. If you watch horses naturally in a group, you can learn much about how they teach each other. The lead horses can walk wherever they want, and the other horses better get out of their way. If they do not, the lead horse will pin their ears, and if the other horses do not catch onto the cue, they bite or kick them until they move out of their way. Horses understand this physical pressure. It is quick, but if they do not notice the slightest cue of an ear or a step in their direction, then the punishment is swift and sharp to follow.

When horses are the happiest, there is no pressure on them, and they are with the herd grazing. When pressure comes their way in the form of a predator, they move away from it. Moving away from pressure is an important concept when training horses. When training horses, we apply pressure and release it once the horse moves away from it. Moving away from pressure is one of the most basic understandings bred into horses. It is also our greatest tool as a trainer to communicate in a way that makes sense to the horse.

The next big concept when training horses is consistency. Through consistently drilling an idea, the horse will soon figure it out. Combined with repetitions, you make the wrong thing hard and the right thing easy. Horses are habitual, so if you never let them do it the wrong way, they will not develop bad habits. If you know a program all the way through it is easier to avoid these issues that can turn into big problems. Many new trainers struggle to with this concept because they are training in the moment not knowing where they should end up. It would be like building a house without the blueprints.

Now, this does not even explain how a horse works off its lateral, how we must get the head correct to get the feet right. I understand I have yet to explain step by step how to build a spin, a reverse arch, a lateral, a soft feel, or a sliding stop. But those few concepts are the building blocks of all those maneuvers. Most of the time, if the horse is not doing the correct step, we must properly set them up. To be a great horse trainer, you have to have the connection from your hand to the rein, to the horse's face, to the horse's feet, and finally to the release of pressure. The pressure release tells the horse that they did a good job. When the pressure is released, the horse is the happiest, not by petting the horse but by removing the pressure.

I was quickly learning all of these new things about horses and how to train them. Each horse I trained made me better understand the next horse. My rodeo horses were turning out better. Most people could recognize the calmness in the horse's eye and the willingness the horse had to do their job.

I was at a branding in college, and this older gal made this comment to me. This older gal said, "I do not know what it is, but there is something different about your horses. They seem never to make a wrong step, and your horse is always ready to make the correct step before you even go into the herd. The thing that is so amazing is your cues are so small it seems like you are almost doing nothing at all."

That was one of the biggest compliments I received, and it let me know that I was on the right path with my training. This older gal had been around a lot of great horsemen, but she saw something different in the way I handled horses. This older gal could recognize that my horses responded to me.

I have constantly challenged myself with how refined I could make a horse and how small I could make my cues. I compared it to painting. When the painter pays so much attention to detail, you use a brush with one hair. That is a comparable metaphor to what correct horse training should be.

Throughout this book, there will be more talk about training horses, but that will lay enough foundations to understand the next part of the journey. Again, these are three very different topics, but they all lead to the same place. I hope you have enjoyed the journey to get there so far!

Chapter 3: Rodeo

RODEO

My adrenaline would be pumping. At this point, adrenalin would run through my veins at full force. Top athletes know the feeling. It is like the moment before battle. There in front of you sits the opportunity to win, in all its glory, or to be busted up and destroyed. Then the announcer would holler out my two favorite words, "LETTTTS ROOOODEOOO".

I get chills and goosebumps thinking about it still to this day. Some of my earliest childhood memories I can remember watching rodeo on VHS and listening to cowboy music. I did not even care for cartoons that much growing up. Don't get me wrong, I watched a few here and there, but if there was a rodeo or a cowboy movie on the TV, that is what I would be watching. I remember watching steer wrestling and thinking to myself that is the event I am going to do. Even as a kid, I remember thinking steer wrestling was a beautiful dance, eloquent in its design, mixed with man, beast, and muscle. It was the tough man's sport. Not that the bull and bronc riders were not equally as tough, but steer wrestlers were the kind of tough that no one messed with. They were the big guys of rodeo. Steer wrestlers are the ones you want in your corner if a fight breaks out. They were the John Henneries of the rodeo.

On the other hand, saddle bronc was the classic event. Saddle bronc is what started rodeo. Two guys in a round pen were putting a bet on who could ride the rank horses on the outfit. The skill of staying on the rank horses was what the cowboys admired. Cowboys will find themselves many miles from home when a young horse might spook at a bit of wire, a tumbleweed rolling by, or who knows what. If you get bucked off out in the big country, it can make for a long walk back home. Anyway, all the other events are extraordinary, but steer wrestling and saddle bronc riding were the events that caught my eye. The guys who can ride at the top level in these events created poetry in motion. They were the ones that captured my dreams.

I started rodeoing when I was in middle school. The North West Junior Rodeo circuit is where I got started. They had a handful of rodeos throughout the summer. The Peninsula Junior Rodeo Association held practices that I would go to. Even in middle school, I often felt I had a late start compared to the kids I was competing against. That did not stop me from working as hard as I possibly could. It might have been two or three years of competing before I won my first buckle. I covered my steer for six seconds and won my first buckle at the Enumclaw Junior Rodeo. After that, I lost track of the buckles I won. I was a Senior in Junior rodeo before I won my first all-around title. The first saddle I won was from my local rodeo, and I was very proud of that. I would later win another all-around saddle and some other all-around titles. When I was a Junior in high school, I started high school rodeo.

High school rodeo is where I learned what it meant to become the next-level competitor. My folks would only let me team rope, calf rope, and steer wrestle. In junior rodeo, we only had chute dogging, which left the jumping off the horse part out of the equation. It was a safer way to get a feel for throwing steers. I remember at practice getting ready for high school steer wrestling. I ran my horse past a couple of steers to build up my confidence. After I ran past the third or fourth steer, it felt good, so I jumped off and grabbed a set of horns. The steer was big. When I jumped on the steer's head, it was strong enough to keep its head up and run with me still hanging onto it. The steer ran to the end of the pen without my feet even touching the ground, but I caught the first steer I ever jumped. Catching the steer excited me. With that catch, I was addicted to the event of steer wrestling. Not knowing what I was doing, I started jumping steers at the high school rodeos. Soon, people began to notice my ability to catch steers. It did not take long, and some of the greatest steer wrestlers were helping me along the way at different rodeo schools.

Now, I have to take a side note in the middle of this section and remind you how my social life was going back home. NOT GOOD AT ALL. Kids were still bullying me. At my big school, I had one friend, and I was one of the biggest targets. I remember a new kid came to our school, and we started to be friends. For some reason, my classmates convinced him that I was a loser, and if he hung out with me, he would be a loser, too. In the middle of PE class, he decided to prove to me that he was no longer my friend, and he pulled down my gym shorts in front of everybody. The only problem was he managed to grab a hold of my boxers, too. I was mortified. I was left standing there exposed in front of my whole class. My classmates, all pointing and laughing at my lack of development, left me there standing and crying.

It was a confusing time in my life. On the weekends, I was one of the cool kids. During the week, I was one of the biggest losers in my school. I used the energy of anger inside me to try and prove them wrong. It was great fuel to encourage me to work harder and my way of handling the emotional pain. I tell people that I thought I was wrong, but it turns out that I was just in the wrong place. I felt that no one could love me for who I was. It turned out that living in a rodeo town would show me that I was wrong. There was nothing wrong with me. I did not think the same way other people did that I was living around. When I moved away, that aspect of my life got better.

So, back to rodeo, I was starting to thrive! I was in my happy place, and it made me desire rodeo even more. In high school rodeo, the idea of a rodeo family became true to me. Other parents would support and help all of us kids. My parents made friends with the other rodeo parents, and I enjoyed seeing that as well.

That year, I qualified for international rodeo in team roping and calf roping. We traveled down to Fallen, Nevada. When I got there, I was amazed by the amount of people there. There were people from all the major rodeo states and even competitors from Canada and Australia. In the first go, I ended up catching in the team roping. My partner and I had a shot at maybe placing nationally! There were dances every night. You could go from one campsite to another just hanging out and chatting about rodeo. Everyone was friendly, and no one had their guard up. Being at that rodeo was a great time.

I missed the heels on our second steer, which took away our chances of placing. It killed me that my mistake cost my partner the opportunity to rank nationally. But that is rodeo. You are constantly measured every weekend. Sometimes you win, and sometimes you lose. The feeling when you win is addicting. The highs were high, and the lows were low, but I realized the only way to win is if you are willing to take the risk.

The following year, I qualified for the High School National Rodeo in Farmington, New Mexico. The top three places in their state went to Nationals. I made it in the steer wrestling. At Farmington, it was the middle of their monsoon season. The days would be hot and sunny, and later in the evening, a thunderstorm would roll in. It would rain hard, but it never lasted long. I did not compete well there. My steer wrestling horse was not running by steers. Come to find out, the family that hauled my horse, their kid spent some time team roping on my steer wrestling horse. That teaches the horse to follow a steer instead of running past, which we need in steer wrestling. Nonetheless, it was an incredible opportunity.

Then there was college rodeo! For the first time, I felt like I was on my own. In high school, my dad helped out a bunch. Looking back at it, I do appreciate what he did for me. At that time, I needed to prove to myself that I could do it all on my own. The first couple of rodeos, I didn't invite my folks to watch me compete. I know it was hard on them, but I needed the time to figure out who I was as a person and competitor.

In my first college rodeo, I placed in the Friday rodeo! On Saturday, I qualified for the short go on

Sunday. I managed to place in the short-go as well. I surprised myself with how well I did. In all honesty, I was just excited to get to compete with some of the best! The college rodeo club paid for my entry fees, gave me a little gas money, and we got to keep our winnings. The winnings were small, but as a college student, every bit helped. Since they paid for the entry fees, I competed in every event but bareback riding.

We were at the Walla Walla College rodeo. I was traveling with four gals on the rodeo team. It was the first rodeo that my folks came to. My dad asked me, "What do you want me to do to help?" I told him, "Dad, I want you to sit in the stands and enjoy the rodeo!" Looking back, I know that was hard for him to hear. At the time, it was what I needed. I placed in a couple of events, the steer wrestling and the team roping.

Rodeo cowboys can be superstitious. Some superstitions are: don't put your hat on the bed, leave the tags on a new pair of boots till they wear off, if you are winning in a particular cowboy shirt then continue to wear it, and don't change your rope while it is catching. I never considered myself superstitious, but there was one rule. DON'T TURN THE A/C ON IN THE HOTEL ROOM! It might have been a little superstitious, but from my observations, I got sick every time I slept in a hotel room with the A/C on. I told my traveling partners this rule of mine. I then went to bed, in my bedroll, on the floor of the hotel room. It might come as a surprise to you, but I didn't party back then. I didn't drink. I was taking my rodeo seriously. Occasionally, I would go to parties, but I would hang out and drink my water. Well, my traveling partners went out partying, and I was sound asleep when they came back to the hotel room. One of the gals turned on the A/C. Sure enough, the following day, I woke up sicker than a dog.

When it came time for the rodeo, I still was not feeling well. In the cowboy culture, there is a strong, never give up, never quit, and don't complain attitude. So, we rode on! My first event was the saddle bronc riding. I rode my horse a good handful of jumps, and he bucked me off so hard on my head I was seeing stars. I struggled to find the fence as everything was spinning. I had to hustle over to my steer wrestling horse. In the steer wrestling, I got down in the hole. Getting down in the whole means that I am hanging off my horse by one hand with one foot in the stirrup, and my armpit is on the steer back. While hanging there, you are waiting to catch the head of the steer as your horse runs past the animal. All of this is being done while you're traveling 30 to 40 miles per hour. Before I could make a head catch, my hazer bumped the steer. When he bumped the steer, it twisted me around, and I caught the back of my heels in the dirt. The momentum sent me to hit my head on the hard arena again. The hit on my head knocked me dizzy, and I saw stars. I still had bull riding left. In the bull riding, my bull jumped out three or four jumps, and then he turned back hard to the left. I made it past the first 360-degree spin, and he sucked me down into the well. Being sucked into the well means you have fallen to the inside of the spin and CRACK! I took a horn to the head.

Luckily, I was wearing a hockey helmet. To understand what it felt like, imagine a pro baseball player with a two-thousand-pound bat whacking you in the head. I was messed up and sore and ready for bed. In my college rodeo career, that was the only short go I didn't qualify for. Also, it reconfirmed why you never turn the

A/C on in the hotel room. I wouldn't be surprised if I acquired three different concussions that night. These undocumented concussions will be an essential part to remember later on in the story.

The last college rodeo was down in Pendleton, Oregon. The arena is legendary in the rodeo world. The central part is grass with a dirt track around the outside. They still have the old wood-bucking chutes, and it is one of the oldest rodeos. It was exhilarating to get to compete there. I was sitting well in the standings for steer wrestling. If I did well, I could make it to nationals! I caught my steer on Friday, but I hullahanded the steer. Hullahanding a steer means that my legs come flying off the horse after I make a head catch, and my legs cross in front of the steer, it can trip me up and the steer up. Then, the steer's nose drives into the ground, and they cartwheel. Often, the steer ends up landing on top of you. Hullahanding a steer is also not a legal throw. You have to let the steer up and throw them again, which I did. I placed but could have done better. Also, my heading partner did not show up to the rodeo. I could use another competitor not in the team roping, and we placed. It was incredible to get a paycheck with someone I had never roped with. Saturday, I had a good catch and threw my steer well. I was qualified for the short-go with a good chance of moving up into the standings and qualifying for nationals. Everyone had bucked off in the saddle bronc riding. When Sunday came around, everyone got to get on another horse. To make the arena smaller, they put panels up. Shortening the arena made it easier to get stock out of the arena. Unfortunately, it made it challenging for the bucking horses. The bucking horses had to turn a sharp corner on grass before the eight seconds. Grass can be pretty slick and hard, come to find out.

I crawled onto my bucking horse and nodded my head. I made it to the fence, and I was still on. I knew I was getting close to the whistle, but I was getting pretty loose. When the horse made the left-hand turn, it threw me to the outside of the horse. I dug deep and hung on just a little longer. I heard the whistle blow! I made it, and I covered my bucking horse. I remember letting go of my bronc rein, and the lights went out.

The next thing that I remember, I was waking up in the hospital, mad that they had me there against my will, and I needed to hurry back to get on my steer wrestling horse. They had me strapped to the backboard because they were worried about spinal injury, but all I was concerned about was getting back to rodeo. I was coming in and out still at that time. I talked to my uncle on the phone for thirty minutes, and still to this day I can't tell you a single word I said. It completely wiped my short-term memory out. The worst of all it was it was on Mother's Day. I guess when I partially came to consciousness in the arena, I was screaming bloody murder. I puked a bunch, and I had internal bleeding. Some humor did come out of it, though. The doctor asked me to wiggle my toes, and I told him," I couldn't, but it was okay because I can't usually move my toes." He looked up at my mom and she nodded her head that I was telling the truth. When I was young, I crammed my feet into cowboy boots that were too small. My boots bound my toes, and because of that, I have hammer toes that don't work anymore.

The other funny thing was the internal bleeding. That doesn't sound too funny on the surface, but the doctor was asking about it. The doctor said it was weird because there was dried blood in me as well. Turns out, when I hullahanded the steer, it gave me some internal bleeding that was going on all weekend. When I got in the bronc wreck, it knocked some of the internal bleeding back loose.

I took third place on the horse, but unfortunately, I did not make it to nationals in steer wrestling. That major brain injury completely changed my life. As crazy as it is to say, I am very thankful that it happened. It taught me a lot, and it is the reason for the other two-thirds of this book. We will come back to that some more, but there are still some more college rodeo stories to tell!

After that, the following year, I was back riding again. I was back in Ontario, Oregon; I drew a little sorrel horse in the saddle bronc riding. I got everything ready like I usually do. At that point in my life, it was just another rodeo. I got my horse saddled in the chute, and I climbed down. You always grab your easy stirrup first, then move the horse over to get your other stirrup. I would then ensure my chaps were straightened up and not caught in my stirrup. Then, check my mark on my bronc rein, push myself good and under my swells, lean way back, and lift the bronc rein just a little. Finally, I nod my head! In the first jump, you have to hit your mark out, which means your spurs must be in contact with the horse above the brakes of the shoulders. This horse was bucking well, and it was a light, snappy horse. I felt the timing of the horse's jumps and kicks for the first time, and I was spurring him a bit. It was the first horse that felt good. It felt like I was making a good ride. I was charging upfront with my spurs, and the next thing I knew, I was on the ground before the whistle.

I was pretty bummed because the ride felt so good. What went wrong? As I gathered myself up, I looked down, and my stirrup and stirrup leather had all ripped out. My stirrup leather and stirrup were still on my boot. That had explained it. My quarter bind had broken, which is the strap that holds the stirrup leather onto the tree of the saddle. I fixed it with baling twine, and I was back ready to rodeo again. Suddenly, after my repair job, I started covering more horses. I always rode broncs more like a colt buster, but I was beginning to spur a little here and there.

I managed to qualify for nationals that year. Having the baling twine, I knew I couldn't go to that big rodeo with baling twine holding my stirrup on, so I bought some new quarter binds. While at nationals, the first horse I drew was a big old grey horse. Some of the other bronc riders had mentioned that one of the pro guys had an 88 on him at the pro rodeo the weekend before. He came out bucking hard, and I was giving it my all. He made a big sweeping corner to the left, and just before he made it to the fence, he bucked me off. I tried my best, but I couldn't get it done. The next horse I got on, I was doing pretty good, but before the whistle blew, I lost my stirrup, which made it a no score. I at least made it to the whistle, though, which I was excited about. One of my buddies drew that same grey horse I had in the first round. He didn't even make it to the corner on him. Seeing my buddy struggle with the same horse made me feel better about my effort.

My third horse was a horse of Harold Vold's. Harold Vold's name is legendary in the rodeo world. He often takes several horses to the NFR each year. He was pretty old at that time, and it was his daughter that was running stock for him. Once you find out your draw, then the next thing you do is try and find the stock contractor. Once you find the stock contractor, they can tell you the measure on the rein. Every horse takes something different, depending on how far the horse sticks their head between their legs. On average, you might hear something like x and 2. That means you measure out the standard which is the x. To do that, you hold the horse's head straight, pull the bronc rein tight, and behind the swells in the saddle seat, you make a fist with your thumb sticking out, and that is how you mark your x or your standard. From there, if it is an x and 2, it would be two fingers past the standard mark. This horse was not that tall, and when I found the stock contractor, she told me 2x on the bronc rein. I looked at her and asked if she meant an x and 2 and she replied, "No, a 2x". That was the first time I had taken a rein that long before or even heard of measuring one out like that. Once I had my standard, I measured another standard and crawled on.

When I called for the horse, he ripped out of the chute harder than any horse I had ever been on. He slid some more rein through my hand, and with each jump, he would throw his head back up. When a horse travels that much with their head, it is hard to ride because lifting on the rein helps keep us under our swells. If you have roped the hind foot of a horse when they go to kicking, that is what it feels like. For the non-horse people, it would be like playing tug of war against ten people. Instead of just pulling hard constantly, it is like them bumping hard and giving it back to you. He bucked me off. Never before had I ever had such a small horse buck so hard.

That year that I made it to nationals in bronc riding, all three of our region's contestants in steer wrestling all placed in the top 15. We had a solid region for steer wrestling. I didn't compete well, but I was thankful to get to be a part of the action. I was proud to see my other buddies do well in their events. Many of those competitors would go on to compete in pro rodeo. Several of those competitors went on to placing at the National Finals Rodeo. The NFR tittle is the greatest title that a rodeo cowboy can win.

Another college rodeo story worth telling happened in Colfax, Washington. The Friday night rodeo was wild because it was raining, storming, lightning, and thunder. We still rode on. I caught my steer for steer wrestling, and before I could throw him, he ran me into the chain link fence. It banged me up a little, but nothing terrible. But the next day, in the saddle bronc riding, I was in a bit of a wreck. I climbed on the horse, and I got both my stirrups like I always did, but before I could nod my head, the horse flipped over backward on me. When the horse flipped over, it smashed me against the back of the chute underneath the horse.

Luckily, the gate crew opened up the gate. Somehow, when the horse scrambled to its feet, I was still on top of it. Since the horse had fallen, I had received a free roll. A free roll is when you no longer have to get your mark out. Anyway, I was D up, which means my spurs were back to the back D rings of my saddle. Having your spurs back there locks you in pretty well, but it can be a rough ride. I got the horse covered. I was the only one to cover a horse that day. I won the rodeo and won the average.

From the horse flipping over, my lower back was bruised up badly. I remember lying face down in the bed in the hotel room. My mom said, "Let me look at your back." I pulled up my shirt, and she took a look and said, "Jim, you maybe should get Carl a drink." My dad quit drinking when I was a kid. My mom never drank much, and I did not drink then either, so to hear my mom say that comment made me laugh. The only problem with laughing was it hurt my back. The back injury lasted for well over a year. If I worked my back too much, it would hurt so bad that I couldn't sleep. I did not manage to qualify for the CNFR that year, but I was in the top ten in both steer wrestling and saddle bronc riding.

My final year began well for me in steer wrestling. After a couple of rodeos in the spring, I was leading in the average until Milton-Freewater. This rodeo was different because it was two one-day rodeos. One-day rodeos have double the points for both days. I didn't draw well. I lost the lead and bumped to fourth. I placed more that year, but I need to be better to bump myself into the top three. That is how I finished my college rodeo career.

The memories made, places traveled, and time spent with friends and family, I would never trade for anything. Yes, there were some wrecks, bumps, and bruises, but I enjoyed every minute. If it makes me a sore older man, I am okay with that because I lived my life to the fullest. It taught me confidence, grit, determination, a growth mindset, and compassion. Most importantly, thank you to everyone who helped me along the way!

Chapter 4: Cowboying

COWBOYING

As a kid, all I ever dreamed about was being a cowboy. My first winter, I worked for an outfit in Ellensburg that used to have rodeo stock. I only got a little experience around the cowboy side of things. I mainly chopped wood and helped move panels and other chores needed for the day.

My next job involved fencing and feeding cows. Feeding cows was the first time I had a cowboy job. It lasted through the winter, and I met a good friend. We ended up playing music together, and we still hang out. The only funny story I remember from that place happened one cold winter day. We were feeding big bales. These bales weigh anywhere from 1200 pounds up to 2000 pounds. We had made these special hay hooks. We welded a swather blade onto the back of a hay hook. We then set that into a wood hammer handle. We had invented a tool that looked like a redneck tomahawk. This tool allowed us to cut the bailing twine strings, and when flakes froze together, we could use the hook to help rip the flakes apart. We would cut all but one twine string, so we didn't have to fumble around as much when we got to the bumpy cow pasture.

Well, I had cut all the twine strings but one. I was waiting for my buddy to do something else with the tractor. The bales were on the feed wagon, ready to go. As a bored young dumb kid of 19, I decided to throw my hay hook at the bale and see if I could stick it in the hay. I had a few failed attempts, but the misses showed some potential of my idea working. I was making the appropriate adjustments to get the rotation right. Just then, my buddy came around the corner to see me make my final attempt to stick it. Well, the hay hook went tumbling through the air, and it just about hit the perfect spot to stick, but it hit the only piece of twine holding the whole bale together. When it popped the string, there was nothing to keep the bale together, so about 800 pounds of the 1200 pounds of hay fell to the ground. Unfortunately, it was in the driveway, not the cow pasture where it needed to be. We both looked at each other and laughed, knowing it was a one-in-a-million shot that had just happened before our eyes. That day, I worked some free overtime fixing my screw-up, but we cleaned it up. After that throw, I have never attempted that trick again. Shoveling loose hay was enough to help me learn my lesson.

That summer, I started working for one of my favorite ranches. They would bring in Hawaiian cattle. The Hawaiians would maintain ownership, and we would disperse cattle all over. We got paid for the weight that the animal gained. Working at this ranch is where I learned low-stress cattle handling.

We would ride horses to move cows from pasture to pasture. We did all the cattle doctoring on our horses and with a rope. I loved that pasture roping! I was also a part of their branding crew. They headed and healed everything. Working for that ranch is where I fell in love with branding. The rodeo was fantastic, but the branding pen is where my passion was. Working for that outfit, I was able to be around some guys who could rope well. Through hanging out with these cowboys, this is where I first saw the Vaquero style of horsemanship. It was the most beautiful art I had ever seen. I knew I could learn to train horses that way and still use what I had learned from training in the reining discipline to make some excellent horses.

I loved everything about that job, other than irrigating. I understand the importance of growing feed for the cattle. I just preferred to be riding a horse. With a smaller outfit, you have to do a little of everything. After working for that ranch, I spent several years as a wrangler for a Christian horse camp. I got another cowboy job several years later.

The following summer, I started a new job working for a Christian horse camp. I worked for the Christian horse camp for nine years. I was there when the camp started, and I was there to help my boss sell off all the horses when it ended. I acquired many stories over those years. I will save those stories for a later chapter. At this time real cowboys would not consider my job a cowboy job, but I was still happy getting paid to ride horses.

I entered into a ranch roping competition, and I got paired up with a guy who was new to me. We ended up taking third in the roping. I was happy, excited, and proud of my horse for doing well in the first ranch roping competition. I started cowboying for an outfit in the Sprague area. I met this new boss through the guy I had met through the ranch roping competition. Going out to the ranch between Sprague and Saint John, I had found my heaven. The boss of that outfit and I have become good friends, to the point where we now consider each other family. I brand every spring for them and work the fall gathering.

We ride some big country, and everything we do, we do it traditionally. Like the first outfit, being around professional ropers and horsemen is where my heart finds some of its greatest joy. There were some well-trained horses in rodeo, but in the cowboy world, it is different. The connection that some of these great trainers have with their horses, you can see it in how they work cattle. These horsemen try to make every move that much easier on their horse and the cattle. These great horsemen view efficiency as energy, and we want the cow to use all their energy to gain weight or raise the best calf they can.

I believe there is more meaning to the horse working on a ranch than performing in the rodeo arena. In the rodeo arena, you are going fast, but in ranching, the work is much slower. Allowing the work to go slower for your horse, you can be more aware of how you set your horse up to do the job. It is the difference between speed reading and when you land that first book that you want to hang onto every word. The actual great ranchers are pushing towards efficiency at every level. The better you set your horse up, the fewer steps they must take. Fewer steps for your horse can be necessary at the end of a long day. You need every step they give you to go in the right direction. Moving your horse less, sets the cattle up to move the least amount as possible. We only want to work cattle as much as we have to because every muscle they move burns calories. As cattle ranchers, we want all the cow's calories to produce the best calf possible and all the calf's calories to produce the best meat possible.

Also, if you rope and handle cattle well, you make it much easier on your ground crew. They, too, only have so much energy to give, and maximizing how we work our horses and the cattle also makes their job easier. We are all friends in the branding pen, so if I can do extra work on my horse to make my buddy's job more manageable on the ground, he will greatly appreciate it.

I will describe what branding is like for someone who does not know. It starts first with the gathering. Depending on the size of the pasture, this can take a couple of hours to get done. The country at my buddy's ranch is big, rocky, and has many hiding holes. The cow has the advantage. We can get the job done with four or five good cowboys. You start by riding to the back of the pasture. You drop people off at different spots depending on where the cattle might try and duck out. Then, you slowly start bumping cattle in the direction you want the cattle to go. Depending on how wild the cattle are, a yip or a smack on your leg is enough to get them to move in the right direction. Pretty soon, you have a herd. The people on the sides must pay attention to those in the back. They are in charge of guiding the cattle from side to side. They can turn the herd back on itself if they get too far in front of the cattle. If the cattle know the routine, it can go smoothly. They can try to split back on you if you have new cattle. For whatever reason, gates can be tricky. The cattle will ball up until one of the cows can figure out where to go. The cattle can mill around and try to bust back past the riders on the gather. It's a delicate balance between pushing them hard enough to where they will move through the gate but not pressing so hard that you scatter the herd.

Once we get them all in the branding trap (usually a big square pen), getting the irons hot and all the vaccines ready to go takes some time. The time for the irons to get hot is perfect because you want some time for the cattle to settle before you start roping. You then have different people to do all the jobs. The ground crew consists of a few tough guys who will tail the animal to the ground, and then they will set the ropes. Setting the ropes starts by pulling the loop around the neck off and putting the rope over the two front feet. If a guy only roped one hind leg, the ground crew will pull the rope and put it on both hind legs. Having the calf stretched between two horses by the ropes allows us to hold the calf down safely while doing all the other necessary jobs. The jobs include branding, vaccinating, castrating, and doctoring.

The ropers try and pick the calves first that are hanging out on the outside of the herd. Once a person has them roped around the neck, he will follow the calf to get short on their rope. Getting short on the rope allows for a better handle for the heeler and less of a chance of wrecks once you are around your ground crew. They then drag the calf out of the herd at a slow trot or faster if the calf is traveling. You always want to keep constant pressure on the calf and keep him traveling in a straight line. Keeping the calf traveling straight and at a constant speed will give your healers the best chance to rope clean. One guy will ride high on the calf to help keep them from squirting, and the other guy rides in for a heel shot. The calf might only be a few minutes off the cow if everything goes well. A good cowboy will try to make it as easy on the calf and ground crew. Roping calves in this manner allows us to work three to four calves at a time. We can easily beat a calf table if we have a good ground crew and an excellent roping crew because we can work multiple calves simultaneously.

Many people think branding is cruel to the animal, but branding has an essential purpose. A brand mark is the only mark that maintains proof of the original mark. Even if the brand is altered or branded over the top of the old brand. When you skin the animal, you can still tell the original mark. Branding your cattle is vital because people will steal cattle. Some people will tattoo cattle on their lips. If a cow's lip tattoo is changed, you cannot tell once it heals. The same goes for ear tags. Ear tags can be removed and changed. Some ranches have even tried implanting little microchips under the animal's skin, but if the person who has stolen the cattle has a chip reader, they can cut the microchip out.

Another benefit to branding is on the big outfits, you might share fences with a couple of other ranches, and if an animal gets out, we can get them back to the proper place. Another way to look at how we handle calves is that they are not any different than a human baby. Yes, it might hurt for a second when they get stuck with a needle, but it is for their good to help keep them healthy and safe!

Once we have finished working the calf, the ropers will look at each other, nod their heads, and pop their dallies. Once you pop your dallies, the calf can get up and head back to their momma. Then, we will repeat the process until every calf has a brand on it. After that, we will push the cattle out, and as they leave the pen, the boss will get a head count.

After all the work is done, we cook a big dinner and feed the whole crew. When branding for another outfit, you don't get paid for your work, but you get fed! I have known a few cowboys that if the grub isn't good on an outfit, they won't return to work the next time. In a way, it is an unspoken trade. I will put my energy into your ranch in the form of work, and you put your energy into me in the form of food.

After that, we will sit around a campfire and tell stories. Someone might have a guitar, and we might sing a few songs. Most of the talk is about how the job went, what we could have done better, and horses. Each cowboy will often have a bag of things he is willing to trade. Each guy will get his bag out, look around, and see if they can make a trade. It is a simple and honest existence, but it makes a cowboy a cowboy, and that is what I enjoy being around.

Chapter 5: Working For A Christian Horse Camp

WORKING FOR A CHRISTIAN HORSE CAMP

I was in a bible study group back when I was in college. A group member asked me, "Have you heard about this Christian horse camp deal looking to hire some people?" I said, "No and asked what it was about?" They told me, "They are looking for someone that can rope, ride, and be a cowboy." I thought I was pretty good at those things and better check into the job.

I got the number from somebody and called them up. They informed me that they would love to meet me. Some days later, I drove to the top of the canyon. It looked like some good cowboy country, with sagebrush and few trees. I pulled into a beautiful log cabin. As they answered the door, a bunch of dogs came running out. They greeted me with smiles and invited me in. They were and are some of the kindest people I have ever met. We discussed horses, cowboying, and their plans for the horse camp. I was interested in the job, and they were interested in me. I started for them the very first year that they were open. I initially built many fences for them, and we had a few campers.

We got the horses from a place in Montana, and it was a pretty cool deal. He showed up in a big semi-stock truck and trailer. He backed up to a hill and jumped the horses out of the trailer. The next day, we caught and topped all the horses. The gentleman figured me a pretty good rider as he told me about all the horses and what he knew about them. He picked the guitar that night, and we had a good time.

The first summer was slow, but we had a couple of weeks of campers, and it was a good job. I will not drag it on too long, but I must tell some of my favorite stories from working up there.

We had a gal working for us, and she was one of the gals worried about looking pretty. She never concerned me much, but I probably drove her crazy. I would get a shower every day, but to pack light, I might wear a pair of clothes two or three days in a row. The paper was coming up the next day. The boss told us that the local paper wanted to take pictures and write an article about the camp. This gal informed us that evening that she was a model and was excited about the photo shoot.

The next day, I wore the same clothes I had the previous two days and started doing my morning chores. The chores included feeding horses, watering horses, catching horses, saddling horses, and getting ready for the day. It had been a good three hours of doing chores when I returned to the rec center. When I got there, some of the other workers were laughing, and when I inquired about the happenings, they informed me that the one gal still hadn't made it out of the bathroom. She was in the bathroom, still getting dolled up. We all finished our breakfast when the newspaper people arrived. We asked them what they wanted us to do, and they said to do what we usually do. So, I saddled up an extra horse for them and we took them on a trail ride. They were friendly, and click, click, the camera went, but I never really thought much of it.

A few days later, the local news published the article in the paper. The gal that spent so much time getting ready, raced to get the first copy. The gal had so much joy and excitement on her face, and it was all whipped away like a whiteboard eraser cleaning up the last math problem. With a fake smile, she looked at me and said, "Here," as she handed me the paper. There I was on the front page. There were other pictures of the kids roping and the trail ride. She was in one picture, but she was riding in the back, and it was blurry. We all got a good little chuckle from that. The following story involves the same gal.

It was just me, the counselors, and the boss out riding. We were about two hours on a ride when rain and thunder suddenly started. The skies opened up, and it was a down poor! I Hollard back to the boss and asked him if he wanted me to long trot the crew out of there and he gave me the go-ahead. So, I started trotting my horse down the trail. I looked back just as he yelled back at me to pull up. The counselors bounced from side to side, holding onto the saddle horns and barely staying on. I brought everything back down to a walk and accepted that I would get soaked that day.

We had to ride down this steep hill to make it home. It was a bit sketchy, even for someone who has ridden a bunch, but it wasn't bad. Well, halfway down the hill, she informs us that her saddle is starting to slip. By this time, the saddle was halfway over the horse's neck. She asked me what to do, and I told her to step off the horse. As she did that, she stood straight up and fell forward instead of stepping down. She went thudding down the hill. Her falling spooked her horse, and the horse went running home. I took after the horse. I was on the horse's trial. I found a rein, a stirrup, a saddle blanket, then the saddle, and finally, the horse back at the ranch. I put the horse up in a safe place and rode back out. I found the whole crew, but they had yet to make it far. My boss was getting her up on his horse. The horse, in slow motion, walked under a tree. As she leaned back to avoid the branches, she fell off again. Luckily, that horse didn't run off, but I told my boss maybe she should walk home.

I finally got everyone back to the ranch and out of the rain. I went to collect all the saddle parts. I made it back to the ranch about an hour later and it was still raining hard. Luckily, one of the gals had made coffee, which I enjoyed as I was soaked and cold from the day. The gal piped up. She said, "Well, that was my first." I asked her, "What was her first?" She said, "It was my first time getting bucked off!" Without missing a beat, I said, "You know a horse has to be bucking first before you can get bucked off. What you did was just fell off." Everyone but the gal started laughing.

One of the most impressive stories I remember from camp started pretty ordinary. We had a typical day of riding horses, doing chores, and feeding. We had dinner, hung out briefly, and headed off to bed. The next thing I heard, at almost midnight, was one of the counselors yelling into my wall tent, "Horses are out. What do we do?" I sprung up. I always slept in my jeans just in case something like this happened. I rallied the troops and assigned everybody their jobs. I sent one gal to tell our boss and said a different gal to wait at the gate. I told her, "No matter what, don't leave the gate!"

Another gal I said to follow the horse tracks and let us know if they were going down the road or up it! The other wrangler and I saddled our horses. We kept our horses in separate pens and headed out at a trot. The gal tracking the horses did a great job and said they were heading down the road. It was a good couple of miles down the road when we found them. I told the wrangler gal that they were going to spook. She rode a mare. I told her she would have to get out front, and I would turn the herd. Sure enough, just as I said, the horses picked up their heads and bolted. I spurred my horse up, got behind them, and turned them up the road.

The horses were in a dead run, and the wrangler gal was stuck in the middle of the herd. Being surrounded by forty horses running is dangerous, but she kept riding through the herd. She ran her horse right through to the front and took the lead. Just as we got to the driveway to turn the horses in, my boss pulled out in his pickup with the headlights on. I thought to myself, we are going to lose the herd. The wrangler gal didn't miss a beat. She rolled around the boss's truck, and the forty horses and mules followed her. I can't even imagine the sight that must have been for my boss sitting there in the front seat. He had never been around cowboying, just packing. I know he has never run a herd of horses.

The wrangler gal rode across the bridge and into the pen. We closed the gate, and we had all but one mule in. Luckily, the mule was kind, and the boss caught it and finished the job. We looked at the clock and managed to finish the whole deal in thirty minutes. The bravery that the wrangler gal showed that night still impresses me! I don't know if she knew how dangerous that ride was, but she was the kind of gal who, if she knew the job to do, would get it done. She got it done that night!

The final story I will tell in this chapter starts with a gal who likes to play practical jokes on people. At this point in my career with this outfit, it was well-established that you didn't mess with me. A lot of the time, I was running the horse side of things and also being a counselor. I was up until 10:00 at night. Many mornings, I would be up at 3:30 to get ready to feed the horses. She was joking about pranking people and how much fun she thought it was! I told her, by all means, have your fun, but leave me out of it. For some reason, people are attracted to what they can't have. Some people also have to learn the lesson the hard way.

We would all head to the arena and sleep under the stars on Thursday night! It was pretty cool, and the kids enjoyed it. I had to get up early like usual. I would leave my bed rolled out until after I fed horses because it would take a bit for the dew to dry out. Waiting till the sun came out would keep me from having a wet bed the next night. It was all business as usual. When I returned from the morning chores and put my bed away, some-one had decided to spray cheap girl perfume on my pillow. I caught a whiff, and I knew who had done it. When I came around, she was all giggling. Thinking she was quite a prankster and the winner, I let her go about her day leaving her with a flat smile that told her she had screwed up with me.

On Fridays, she was always the first one off the mountain. So, the next week, I devised the perfect plan. Me and another guy waited until everyone went to sleep, and then I got my big truck jack out and a handful of wood blocks. We jacked her little car as far off the ground that our redneck engineering would allow. The next day was Friday. She woke up and came down to the rec center, full of laughs. She thought it was a great prank. After breakfast and everyone got their laughs, she wanted us to help her get her car down. That is when I got the real laugh. I informed her that it was her problem to figure out. That was the first Friday she was the last to leave the ranch. She also learned not to mess with me anymore.

Luckily, my boss took pity on her and helped get her car down. He also struggled with how high we got her car. His jack wouldn't reach, but he was wise enough to figure out how to get her car down. Luckily for her, her car was small, and he could use the tractor to lift it down. I felt terrible that he had to help her, but he understood the lesson that she needed to learn.

I worked for that boss for eight summers at the Christian horse camp. He got in a bad mule wreck late in the summer of that 8th year. The wreck caused him and his wife to shut the camp down. He hired me another summer to help him sell all the horses. My best friend helped me out. We rode daily, training the receptive horses and keeping the others in shape. We managed to sell all the horses that summer. The last sale came on the last weekend of the summer for us. The guy ended up buying the last two horses we had. It was a great way to end the job. I could not have worked for a better family. They became family to me. I had their back and worked my best for them. They knew it and greatly appreciated me! Being appreciated made the hard days worth it for me!

Chapter 6: College

COLLEGE

For having such a horrible high school experience, college was drastically better. I enjoyed it. Being able to go rodeo, meet new people, and experience life's freedom was incredible. I started in pre-dentistry, and I was doing well! I started researching dental schools, but they were all in big cities. I have never liked big cities, and I could not give up my horses and dogs for four years to do that. Two years into college, I decided to be a math teacher. There are several stories I must talk about from college. These experiences have shaped me into the teacher that I am now.

I was taking a class in environmental studies. This class had three different teachers. Two of the teachers did an outstanding job, but I disagreed with the third teacher's approach to presenting science. Science is theories that we observe, and we use the observations to make predictions. Every story has two sides; you should present both sides with as little bias as possible. Students are responsible for not accepting what the teachers offer them as absolute truth. One must first ask oneself; does this make sense? If it does not make any sense, then there is nothing wrong with bringing that up in class. Being fearless in bringing differing ideas up is how we find discoveries through diverse ideas. Science can only make revolutionary discoveries, with people questioning what was previously thought true.

The professor that I did not prefer was teaching global warming as if it were an absolute and not as if it were the current theory. So, I started the challenging discussion I knew he didn't want to have. He was showing a graph that made global warming look like it was on an exponential curve. The problem with an exponential curve is that the last point looks extreme. So, I asked him how he knew that his units were right on the x-axis or that the exponential model best represented what was happening. I already knew enough about math to have a little fun with this. He pathetically stumbled upon an answer about how it is computer generated, and that is just how it is supposed to be. I needed to find a better answer. I pressed it further, and he asked me what I proposed. In front of a class of 150 students, I walked to the front of the class, grabbed the marker from the teacher, and proceeded to teach the class about the concept in calculus called local linearity. It looks like a straight line if we zoom in enough on any curve. If we zoom out using larger units on the x-axis, the scary-looking exponential curve looks like a straight line or just a little spec on the graph.

He came to class the next day with a lesson on how to lie with statistics. I informed him that he did not understand what I was trying to teach him. As a professor, you should teach both sides of the story! Instead of trying to scare people with scary graphs, why don't we use that energy to try and innovate ideas to solve the problem? It would be better than spending that money on generating these graphs that may or may not be telling the actual story.

I was not his favorite by any means. We were then assigned to write an essay explaining our thoughts on science. I brought up the idea that science has been wrong every time in the past; why in the world do you think science is right now? Don't get me wrong, I enjoy science, but science is a tool, not a religion.

The following story takes place in teaching students of ethnic diversity class. The teacher informed us that he was a First Nations Native of Canada. The course started with how all of the native's problems were because of the white man. I took a bit of offense to this because I was white, and I couldn't remember doing anything to make any native's lives more difficult.

At this point, I was pretty versed in the history of the American cowboy. I loved reading the journals of the men who pioneered cattle into the big herds. I was not there to witness it myself, but I know there were conflicts between the natives and the cowboys. I won't even judge who was right or wrong, but I can tell you that mean and brutal things were done on both sides.

I asked the teacher, "Why don't you tell the whole story?" He asked, "What do you mean by that?" I explained, "You have been telling the students about all the mean things whites did to the natives." I asked, "Would you be willing to tell the class all the mean things that the natives did to the whites?" He responded, "You just don't understand because you grew up white privileged!" That was the first time I had been accused of growing up with white privilege! From my view of things growing up poor, white, and in a reservation town, I had not experienced much of this white privileged thing that he was talking about. I told him, "You just made one hell of a claim and, by all means, tell the class where I grew up." He didn't have an answer. He said, "I don't know where you grew up." I explained, "That's right, you have no idea where I grew up, and you have no idea how I grew up. I am only asking if you are going to tell the story; please tell both sides."

The things done in the past were not morally right, but that is how it was. It is easy to fall prey to ethnocentrism. Ethnocentrism is how we can connect to the past, but you should recognize your biased perspective while building your understanding. If you want to fix a problem, it is better to look forward to solutions than to look backward to place the blame. Blaming a group for a problem doesn't fix it. It just breeds more hate and contention between the two parties.

Those examples are some of what I perceived to be wrong with universities. Some professors would place their political bias into their teaching. I never respected when professors taught with their opinions instead of being factual. Considering all that, I also had some great teachers who truly inspired me and were examples of what I wanted to be.

I had one such teacher. He was teaching the history of mathematics. I was apprehensive because history is often presented with a politically biased interpretation. At the start of class, in walks a short little mousey guy. His hair was thin and long on top of his head. His facial hair was scraggly, and he looked like he just crawled out of a dryer. When he started talking, his voice was a high pitch, and he raced through the words. He knew so many great things and was genuinely excited to share his ideas with the class. He instantly dazzled the class with his brilliance and enthusiasm. He was one of the most intelligent professors that I came across. He spoke multiple different languages. He was versed in history, mathematics, psychology, sociology, and science.

We had chapter readings that he would assign. He would give quizzes on the different chapters. I read the chapter I was assigned and then took the quiz. I failed it. I asked to talk to him after class, and he agreed. I explained that the grade I received didn't accurately reflect what he had asked us to do. I explained that I had read the chapter like he had asked us to, but I didn't remember the details that the quiz questions were on. He asked me to explain what I read. I gave him an excellent explanation of the chapter. He said, "Would you rather do a one-page report on what you have read instead of the quizzes?" I agreed to do the reports and received A's on them. I later found out that he changed his class after me. He now allows students to take a quiz or write a one-page reflection. He also admitted that the reflections measured students' comprehension far better than the quizzes.

He inspired me to memorize 100 digits of pi. Weekly, I would write how many numbers I had remembered before class. He would walk in and check my work and fix any mistakes. By the end of the quarter, I accomplished my goal. I would later learn a way more efficient way to do that same task, but I was learning and challenging myself, and he recognized that and encouraged it!

Chapter 7: Deciding To Become A Teacher

DECIDING TO BECOME A TEACHER

As mentioned, I started college thinking I wanted to be a dentist. When I realized being a dentist wasn't a good option, I started reflecting on what I wanted to do. I had been tutoring a bit in science and math since I did well in those classes. There was one gal in particular that I remember working with.

She was on the soccer team. Math was about to prevent her from being able to play. She was in 100-level math and brought her homework to the library, where we met for her first tutoring session. She struggled for about thirty minutes as I watched what she was doing, but I didn't say anything. After working for thirty minutes, she looks up and says, "I do not know how to work with fractions." I told her, "I am well aware, but it was okay. I will help you learn how to work with fractions."

I started out helping her 3 to 4 times a week. I was working with her once a week in the next math class she took. The following math class she took, I helped her once a month. The last class that she had to take in college was pre-calculus. She called me once at the end of the quarter to help her out. I showed up, and she told me correctly how to do all the problems. I informed her, "I think you are ready for the final!" She ended up getting an A- in the class. She was very proud of herself, and I was also proud of her. That experience made me realize I wanted to be a math teacher.

Another part of wanting to become a teacher was fixing all the hypocrisy I observed in school. I wanted to improve the system. I hated when teachers told me not to be on my phone; then they were on their phones. I hated English teachers telling me to read a book when they had not read a book in the last ten years. Many of these teachers have become so detached from their education that they forget the amount of brain energy it takes to learn something. They ignore the importance of fun in learning. I wanted to help students learn. I tried to make the process of learning better for students. They might still not like math after I am done teaching, but I hope they learn more about themselves from the class. I hope my students will learn what methods of studying help them the most. Many teachers made math way more confusing than it needed to be. I want my students to know how they learn, and I want them to have fun accomplishing great learning!

When I finally made that decision, I was terrified to admit it to anyone. I thought I was quitting on my big goal. I feared people would know I hated school and think of me as a hypocrite. "You know the ones that can Do and the ones that can't Teach!" They make little money. So, I tried it out on my grandma. I told her I was considering being a teacher to see her reaction. She looked at me and explained that she thought I would be a great teacher. I was expecting a different answer.

I then told my family and finally declared my major. Surprisingly, they all offered me the same support that my grandma did. It is a weird feeling when you admit something that others have seen in you for longer than I had entertained as a notion. I can only imagine it when Lewis and Clark came across this nation. They saw animals they had no idea of and named them. I had established my professional identity, and my name would be a Math Teacher. Once I spoke that idea into existence, all the paths came together and made sense.

My academic approach completely changed after that. I truly felt God had revealed the path he wanted me to go down. My stress of doing well in my classes had vanished. If this is what God wanted me to do, then he would make things work! He cared for me and put things in place that I had no control over.

At the time, getting into one of the local school districts for student teaching was a lottery. Most kids returned to their hometown, but that was not my option. I had horses and a dog then, and relocating wasn't easy. Luckily, I got into the Ellensburg school district.

I could see the connection between training horses and training people. Training horses and teaching math all involved learning, and I realized how much I enjoyed it. I realized it did not matter if I was teaching a horse, a dog, or a person. I wanted to help make the process easier and more fun! Some of the ideas I had learned from training horses related to teaching people. Build their confidence. Start small and reward the slightest correct effort. Always end on a good note. Show them how before you demand them to do it correctly. Make the right thing easy and the wrong thing hard. They have to repeat the correct action three times before I consider that they might have learned it.

Understanding what they learned yesterday might be challenging today. In academia, we call this an emerging concept. It was like I had a puzzle of a thousand pieces, and they arranged themselves before my eyes. I could see the connections and how it all applied. I realized that learning about teaching would make me a better horse trainer, and training horses would make me a better teacher. If a concept couldn't be applied back and forth, then I questioned its validity. Horses taught me the most honest form of learning. A horse will never lie to you. When a horse needs your help understanding a concept, they will show you. If they are hurt, they will show that they are lame. If they know a concept, they will perform it. Consistency with a cue will create a consistent outcome.

The teacher I was doing my student teaching with was a horse guy doing high-country packing. We got along excellent. I enjoyed the experience of student teaching with him. I was teaching the first week of my student teaching. I appreciated being able to teach. The students challenged me at times, but we made it through, and some of them also learned some math in the process!

Once I finally accepted what I was going to become. My life had more purpose. My life had direction, and I felt like I was starting a journey of a thousand miles. It was daunting and exciting all at the same time. The more I learned about teaching, the more excited I got. To this day, I still get eager to learn about things that involve education. Later in life, I realized that reading a book about building stronger relationships could help me be a better teacher. You can learn how to be a better teacher from sources that were not written with teachers directly in mind. Through understanding people more, I could become a more effective teacher. I love watching good teaching and figuring out what makes it great. I love watching lousy teaching and figuring out how to improve it. Then, find a way to teach the teacher so that the person is encouraged to do better and not discouraged. If you listen to the top chefs, they talk about the first thing they cooked, and it was like their world was whole all of a sudden. A race car driver can recall the first time they got behind the wheel and went fast, and they were addicted. As a horse trainer, you remember the first concept you taught a horse. The first time, you picked up a feel with a horse and released the pressure at the perfect time.

I was going to become a math teacher and was excited to start.

Chapter 8: Learning About Teaching

LEARNING ABOUT TEACHING

The content was familiar to me in the classes I took in college in the education major. Horses had taught me how to teach and what learning looked like. The courses taught me the academic vocabulary of the content I already knew. It was fun, though. It made sense to me, and I connected well with it.

I enjoyed learning child psychology. They mainly talked about the Stage Development Theory by Jean Piaget. One of the concepts of stage development theory is that you will encounter a problem in each stage. You will proceed to the next level of maturity once you resolve the problem. This theory had parallel truths with horses. The babies are curious and investigate things. When they get afraid, they retreat to their mom. As one and two-year-old's, they are developing their sense of play with other horses. They are learning how their body moves and how to get what they want. In this period, they tend to hurt themselves a lot, and physical pain tells them that they went too fast or tried too hard. When they come into training, three-year-old horses start to learn how to resist their biology. Instead of running or fighting what scares them, they must learn to face the problem. Some of these traits directly mirror the development of a student. Most 7th-grade classes have students who tear apart paper and pencils. They have a stage where they are destroying things. It can be frustrating as a teacher, but when you realize it is their way of understanding the object, it can help you manage the behavior. Teenagers are also learning how to build their confidence away from their parents. Teenagers build their confidence by being rebellious, it is a natural process of youth growing up. As teenagers navigate drama and life, they are learning how to get what they want and need.

I enjoyed this psychology class but knew there was more to the story than what was taught. I was curious to learn more about how the brain learns. I was starting to wonder how we can make learning easier. I was beginning to evaluate my teachers. In the purest sense, I was questioning whether they were inspiring me to want to learn. Some teachers made me want to run out of their class. In contrast, other professors had me hanging on their every word. I was starting to break their teaching apart and figure out what was making excellent teaching. I had good examples through college and bad examples of teachers. We often shape how we are as a teacher by how we have been taught. Some academic approaches are shaped by the feelings you have in a class. Other teaching strategies are pulled from research.

Because of my brain injury from rodeoing, I became more interested in how the brain learns. I ask the students if they know how the brain learns? Surprisingly, most students have yet to understand how the brain learns. They have experienced the learning process, but still, the concept is a mystery to them. Not knowing how the brain works is okay, but if we can teach them that learning is not mystical, this can help encourage students to engage in the learning process. Hopefully, they realize that not learning is because they need to repeat or change part of the learning process. Not learning something is not because they are dumb. Understanding how the brain works, will make learning a more enjoyable process. Often, my students will say my classes are easy. It takes less energy to produce more significant results. I am carful with defining my classes as easy because some principals think that if it is easy for students to learn then the class lacks rigor. Yes and no, if we work with the brain and not against it, we will make learning much less painful. My students are able to learn more content. I will get more into that in a later chapter.

While learning about teaching in college, I came across some classes that could have been more enjoyable. The classes on how to write a lesson plan, how to create assessments and classroom management did not excite me as much as some other classes. These classes are the busy work that many students dread. In my professional career, I have never written a traditional lesson plan. The time it takes to do this at the college's standard is far from reasonable in the work world. If you work outside your contracted time and are unpaid, the school is stealing from you. Do not work for free. Your time is worth a lot. Understand your student's time is valuable, too. If you do not work outside of contracted time, do not ask your students to work outside class. There are many reasons, but if nothing else, give them the same respect you deserve.

Creating assessments is easy. Is the assessment measuring what you taught the student? Test the students in the same manner you taught them and in the same way you had them practice. The testing culture for specific subjects is fascinating. It is perfectly okay to show the students the content for some academic subjects. For other classes, similar questions are more appropriate. It would help if you did not trick students on the test. At that point, it is okay to build their confidence a little and show them that they can accomplish the content.

I had a math professor who taught solely in math theory and proofs. The test was entirely on practical application. He was baffled that we all did so horribly. We students explained that we needed to be taught how to apply the theory to practical problems. After he did this, we all started doing tremendously better on the test.

I fought with a professor who would grade my essays based on my writing ability. The teacher did not teach me how to write, so his essays should have been graded on the content that he taught in class. The problem with grading essays on grammar is even English teachers cannot agree on grammar rules. English is a fluid language that changes. English language being fluid is fantastic in the creative side of things because we can change it to fit our needs. It can be troublesome to grade a student on how you believe writing should be if you do not teach them what you are looking for. Even from American to British English, spellings differ, and formal essays are written differently. If you try to write contemporary writing, it breaks so many of the rules a poor high school English teacher would never be able to keep up with the ever-changing styles.

Classroom management is an interesting one. There is a way to teach classroom management to help teachers succeed, but it differs from how the college taught it. It truly depends on what personality that you bring to the table. Myself I have always had a strong presence. So, I can use that presence to my advantage. Every teacher has their advantages. The trick is to learn when to use the talents you possess. If you overuse whatever your strength is, you will weaken its effectiveness. You can be the softest of personalities and still have excellent management. Understand that your leverage bar might be pulling the kid aside, and explain how much you care about them as a person. If you are a soft person, you can show your tough side, but some students might find it funny. You want to rely on something other than that as your main tool. Myself having a more assertive demeanor. I want to rely on something other than that as my only tool for classroom management. I work hard to show the students how caring and compassionate I am. I show the students what kind of grizzly bear teeth I possess, but that should only happen once or twice a year.

Most classroom management issues can be solved by having students work on content and by building positive relationships with them. In that sense, it is not rocket science. The difficulty is learning from the infinite array of personalities. If you approach classroom management in this way, it will work eventually. Never be frustrated by the students, but always be willing to learn from them. My goal is to always convey to the student that my sole care in this world is to help them accomplish their goals. You must understand that achieving their goals could involve reaching a social or academic understanding. I do not believe students are ever born wanting to be failures. They might say they don't care, but this has been conditioned into students. It is challenging for a kid to be mad at you when you start the conversation with, "I care about you and how can we work together on accomplishing....... (insert whatever is needed)."

A class I would create in college to help students learn how to be a teacher would be a class where kids would try to annoy the prospective teacher. If the future teachers get annoyed and snap, they fail the course. If you are easily frustrated by what kids do, you will constantly be frustrated in this profession. If you are annoyed by the students, they will be able to tell and possibly translate this to them thinking that you do not like them. If students feel that you do not like them, they will not perform well for you. These annoying behaviors can manifest in many forms. Tapping a pencil, rocking in a chair, yelling out, and many others, but the question to counteract the frustration that might be building you is, why are they doing it? Is a student rocking in their chair because they have more energy than they can contain? If that is the case, stopping the behavior of rocking in their chair might cause them to blow up in a behavior worse than the annoying behavior.

Your attitude and perception can change the student's behaviors as a teacher. As hard as it might be, you have to remember that you once were a kid. Even if you think you were the perfect kid who never did anything wrong, you must understand that maybe that kid is not you. Also, it may depend on the time of the day. Many times, students might have a burst of energy from what they ate after lunch. I notice depending on what I eat, I feel tired. I feel hyper or do not want to try on a task when I am mentally exhausted. Understand that all the emotions you feel, so do the students. The difference between you and the students is that you can recognize and do something about the feeling. When I am reading, sometimes it makes me tired. If I still need to keep reading, I will get up and read while walking. Reading while standing up counteracts the feeling of tiredness. It is hard to fall asleep when you are walking.

Another class I would have in college would be you show up, and you are given the materials and five minutes to prepare. Having to change your lesson plans on the fly will constantly happen in your career. You will show up thinking you have thirty minutes to get ready, and because of some unforeseen incident, most of the time is spent on some other task. Maybe you have to talk with a student about what is happening in their life. You may go to make copies, the copier is broken, and you spend half the time figuring out how to fix it. The principal may call you in to talk about something that is happening. Regardless, you must create a meaningful lesson that helps students accomplish the next objective. Thinking on the fly gets progressively more accessible the more years you teach a subject. Sometimes, it is a matter of learning how to lose control. This loss of control is not like letting go of a steering wheel in a car crash. It is losing control in the sense that you do not have to control what happens. You can let the things fall into place that life has dealt. Show the kids what you want them to learn and let them find the information out and present it to the class. Allow the student to take ownership in their learning.

Taking classes in college can only teach you so much about teaching. All the ideas that you might have about teaching students will take them and rip them apart and spit them back at you. The best way to learn about teaching is to start teaching. You can learn how to teach by teaching your brother how to build something. You can learn about education by teaching a Sunday school class. You can learn how to teach by training a dog or a horse. You do not have to be in a traditional classroom, but also remember that the closer you practice to how you will play, the better you will play.

Chapter 9: Learning How The Brain Learns

LEARNING HOW THE BRAIN LEARNS

I was thinking about how I would write this chapter. I have read many books on this subject, which I have greatly enjoyed. I will put it into my own words and try to explain it in a way that will make sense to you. I might nerd out for this part of the book, but here we go!

I was taking a sets and logic class in college directly after my brain injury. I was struggling to learn proofs. I told my teacher that I had acquired a brain injury riding a saddle bronc horse, and it was tough for me to learn proofs. I said, "I CAN'T learn proofs." When those nasty words left my mouth, I was instantly disgusted with myself. He replied, "If you can't do it, maybe you should seek help through the school for your handicap." I left that meeting knowing that I needed to figure out how to learn.

I heard one of my buddies talking about this book he read about a guy who learned how to memorize large amounts of information. I asked him what the book was called. It was *Moonwalking with Einstein* by Josh Foer. It blew my mind. He did a great job writing a story and using the research to support his ideas. One of the Ideas that he stumbles across while interviewing these memory champions is that anyone could do it. They challenged him that if he practiced, he too could become a memory champion. The book inspired me! If these tricks worked for him, maybe these tricks for memorizing could work for my damaged brain. I tried the first technique, creating a memory palace....and it worked. Instantly, I was addicted. For the following of this chapter, I will do my best to explain what I learned about the brain and how it might help teachers teach and students learn.

This information came from Moon Walking with Einstein and other books on this topic. At the end of this book, I will compile a list of the books that have helped guide this information and some that I recommend reading.

One misconception that people have is that everyone learns differently. At the cognitive level, that is not true. The process is pretty simple. While reading the book *Brain Rules* by John Medina, he explains what has to happen for learning to have a chance at the cognitive level. The first step is to receive the information in some form or fashion. You can receive the information by seeing how to do it hands-on (kinesthetic), you can receive the information by hearing how to do it(auditory), you can receive the information by taste (gustatory), you can receive the information by smell (part of olfactory). Here is where the misconception starts. You can prefer to receive the information differently, but this is only the first step in the learning process.

People and animals all learn in relatively the same way. When you think about learning between animals and humans, we are using the same organs to achieve learning. Once you have received the information, it goes into your short-term memory. It will last in the short-term memory for about three to five minutes. If we do not access the information from the short-term memory, the brain will get rid of it. Once you access the information from the short-term memory, it becomes a long-term memory. These memories can last thirty minutes to a day, depending on how important you make the memory to your brain. The more you use the new thing you learned, the easier you can access the information, and the longer you can wait between accessing the information. So that is the basics of how we learn.

Interestingly, most teachers and students do not know that, and they even communicate the wrong information. They do it innocently, but they do it nonetheless.

Also, the best way to learn something is in the form that you will be performing the task. You will learn how to throw a football by... you guessed it by throwing a football. You could read all you want about throwing a football and listen to all the greats about throwing a football, but you will only learn how to do that task once you throw a football. In alignment with this cognitive idea, this is why I have a whole chapter titled Learning about Teaching by Teaching.

The next important thing to understand about the brain is that it is a muscle. The beauty in that is by working the brain, we can make it stronger. Understanding that the brain is a muscle is one of the most important pieces I hope teachers will understand and learn about the brain. One of the most basic pedagogical mistakes I see teachers make is trying to teach the students the entire period. Teaching the whole period sounds good in theory, but biologically and cognitively, this idea of how to present learning needs to be corrected. Trying to work a child's brain this way would be like asking an athlete to do push-ups for the entire class period. We can train to get closer to that goal, but most super athletes cannot do push-ups for an hour straight. So, why would we expect students to do that cognitively?

If I wanted to get the most exercise, strength, and conditioning out of an athlete, I might have them do ten push-ups, run for ten minutes, do ten more push-ups, and repeat that process for the hour. Working out this way would be similar to circuit training, a highly effective workout method. Every weight lifter knows you need to rest those muscles the next day before you work them again. Resting your muscles gives your body the time it needs to repair the damaged muscles. So, how can we rest the brain? There are two main ways to do so. The most important way is by sleeping. The second way of regaining brain energy is by letting your brain go into the diffused mode. The diffused mode is where your brain is wondering. So, you might be thinking about what you are going to cook tonight, and then that leads you to think about the kitchen table, and that leads you to think about wood and how you need to finish chopping your wood for the winter and stack it. In diffused mode, your brain stores and sorts the information just like in deep rapid eye movement or REM sleep.

The other mode that the brain performs in is what is called the focused mode. Focused mode is narrow thinking used to solve a problem or learn information. This mode depletes brain energy. Diffused mode helps you come up with creative ideas. Focused mode enables you to concentrate on one task. You can engage students in a creative task or a story to get them into the diffused mode.

So, if I were to create the perfect brain classroom, I would instruct for ten to fifteen minutes, and then for five minutes, students would either draw pictures or move around and exercise. Then, repeat the process. Breaking the class up into sections is a way to build your class in the best way. Also, this allows students to have two or three brain storage times. On the outside, it looks like you're losing ten to fifteen minutes, but cognitively, you are gaining three cognitive store times. Teaching in 15-minute intervals with a break in between will triple the amount of information students can learn in a single period. Just remember what is good for the athlete's muscles will be good for the brain. Give the brain breaks, and don't expect the brain to work for the entire time.

The next critical piece to understand in pedagogical practices is creating cognitive hooks. Cognitive hooks would be like making a reservation for your evening dinner. It creates a place to put the learning when the learning happens. Creating cognitive hooks is a little investment to make learning easier when receiving the information. With a reservation, you know you will have a place to sit when you go there. When you create a cognitive hook, you know you will have a place to store the learning.

An easy way to help create these cognitive hooks is to let the students look through the chapter to examine some of the problems and read some of the information. Pre-reading gives the students a taste test to know what to expect when dinner comes. Another great way to create cognitive hooks is an overview. At the start of the chapter, I will sometimes teach everything quickly. Then, we will spend a day on each of the topics. Finally, the student can create cognitive hooks by making their connection to the learning. Students connecting to the teaching should always be encouraged when they give you a comparative example. Adjust the instance if needed, but try to make that example work with the understanding.

Another fundamental brain psychology concept that should be encouraged in class is celebrating wrong answers. When a student gets an answer wrong, we have an opportunity to learn. If students get an answer correct, they have not learned anything new. The students have regurgitated information that they already know. The tricky question to ask yourself as a teacher is whether my grading encourages students to get wrong answers or punishes them for getting wrong answers. If a student tries on a math assignment, works hard, the assignment is graded, most of the problems are incorrect, and receives a low score, the student then feels punished for trying. It is easy to figure out that the student will stop trying soon after in your class. We always want to reward putting effort into their work. That doesn't mean we don't show the students that they got a problem wrong. It should not hurt their grade to practice a new concept.

Both the reward and punishment are equally important. I have seen conflicting research in that some argue that you will change more behaviors for longer with positive rewards than punishments. But I have seen animals shocked by an electric fence, and even after the fence is not there, they still will not cross the line. That is a vast change in behavior based on punishment.

I have also heard that taking ten dollars from a person for doing a wrong thing will have more of an effect on them than giving them ten dollars for doing the right thing. I will provide you with my information and let you make your thoughts on the subject.

Understanding what the brain likes to remember is vital in making learning more effective. The brain likes to remember weird things. If a man walks downtown dressed like something you have never seen before, maybe they are wearing a baby costume. Without any effort at all, your brain will remember that. The brain's ability to remember weird things is part of why the naked cowboy in New York became a sensation. You remember him for two reasons: one, no one is dressed like him in New York, and two, he has a sexual appeal to people. When you see something weird two hours later, when you get home, you can accurately tell your friend/ spouse what they were wearing, even the most minor details. The brain likes to remember visual things.

I often have students close their eyes and list twenty objects in their house. The students can easily do this. Then I asked them how long they spent studying the house, and most said they didn't. The students just remembered it. Wouldn't it be cool to create the academics so the students can remember it like they remember the things in their house? I believe it can! The brain also loves to remember things of a sexual nature. What it boils down to is if it is weird, it might kill you, so you need to retain it; you need to eat and drink, so you must remember the visual path to and from, and if you do not procreate, that is the end of the species. If we can code the academic content into those categories, it will be more easily remembered by the students.

Now, I must attack another commonly mistaken fallacy: I don't want you to memorize the content; I want you to learn it. This idea's root is good but undermines the biological learning process. Memorization is the first step to learning. So, as a teacher, you shouldn't make memorizing sound like a punitive form of learning. If students learn better ways to remember, they will subsequently have more cognitive energy to process and synthesize the information into their new ideas. The more we can connect a new concept to other ideas we already know, the more likely we will be able to re-access that information.

One of the techniques I use to remember numbers is a coding system. When I read the book Secrets of Mental Math by Arthur Benjamin and Michael Shermer, I learned how to create a code system for memorizing numbers. All of the digits have a letter assigned to them. You can then use any other letter you want to create the word. Changing the numbers into a word allows us to have a visual, and our brains will remember the picture better than a boring string of numbers. So, for my system 1=t; 2=n; 3=m; 4=r; 5=l; 6=sh; 7=k, g, c; 8=f; 9=p, b; and 0=s. So, this might work if I try to memorize the digits of pi, 3.1415926535...... for that first section, it would be trtlbnshlml. Now, that does not work to create a word or a picture. But you can use all the other letters to create words. So, for that sequence of letters, it turns into tire tool banish lemel. In my mind, the picture I am seeing is the tire tool that is banish(ed) from the castle, and left is a pile of metal shavings, which is what lemel is. The cool part with this system is I don't have to spell words correctly. Once you have defined the word in your mind, when you see the picture, you can quickly recall your spelling and decode it. It seems like more work, and there is a little front-loading. Once you learn the system, you can use it for anything. I use this system to memorize my credit card numbers, phone numbers, pi, and any other case that I might need to memorize numbers.

In the book *Moonwalking with Einstein*, Joshua Foer discusses what it takes to memorize a long list of things. I will use a memory palace to learn a list of things where order is important. A memory palace is any house or place you might be familiar with. It is pretty simple. You walk through the place sequentially like you might walk through the house, and you place the pictures in each spot. For pi, I walk up to my grandma's house. I look to the right and see the image of the tire tool banishing, and all that is left is the pile of lemel. Then, when I looked to the left of the front porch, I saw a man lying. He fibs about being a cowboy, but he is just a man. So, the code words for that picture are fib, cowboy, and man. Try it on your own now and see if you can figure out what digits of pi are in the words fib, cowboy, and man. Then, I have a picture attached to her door. I walk in, and to the left, there is another image on her dining room table. I keep going around the house, placing different pictures in different places. One hundred digits of pi fit in my grandma's house just right.

Using those two techniques, I could significantly increase the capacity of items I could remember. Another great strategy is creating an acronym. In this case, each letter of the word stands for a different word. My favorite example of an acronym in math is SOH-CAH-TOA. SOH stands for sin equals opposite divided by the hypotenuse. CAH stands for cos equal to the adjacent length divided by the hypotenuse. Finally, TOA stands for tan equals opposite divided by adjacent.

You can combine an acronym with creating a story with the information you want to learn. The more information you connect with the new concept the easier you will be able to remember it.

If I have math formulas to memorize, I like changing those into pictures. In the book Brain Rules, John Medina explains turning the formula for the volume of a sphere into a picture. I tried it, and it amazed me how easy it was to remember a complex formula. I will teach my students to convert formulas into pictures to remember them better. For example, $y=mx+b$ will turn into a M mountain because mountains have slopes, and M represents the slope. Then, a skier is flying off the slopes, and his skies are crossed in an X. Finally, I have a bumble bee to stand for the B, flying back to the starting point that the skier came from. The bee stands for the starting point or the y-intercept in the equation. Having students create their pictures takes more time, but it will help them increase their ability to remember the formula. Creating these pictures to help remember equations also helps students to develop their creativity. Finally, if students produce their picture to memorize a formula, they will know how to apply this technique to other learning opportunities.

With these techniques, not only are students learning the information or memorizing the information much better, but they are also getting time to practice being creative. Working through learning also gives students a unique education that fits their needs and interests. Teaching them these tools allows them to solve any cognitive learning task they might have. The best part is they can use these techniques in any subject to memorize more efficiently, creating longer-lasting memories. Students will learn more for longer, and it will not be the painful process that they dread.

We know much about the brain and how it learns. Many of these techniques have been used for hundreds of years. We can apply these tools to learning and take the mystery out of learning for students. There is still so much to learn about the brain. The brain is the most complex organ in our body. We can do some straightforward things in the classroom to increase significantly the effectiveness of the content learned. If we teach students how their brain works, this will empower students to investigate it themselves. If they try one memorization technique that works for them, they will be more likely to try that same technique on different content. The more they use a system, the more it will happen effortlessly. Students will step away thinking wow, that was easy without realizing the amount of content and the depth of content they accomplished. If we as teachers practice these memorizing techniques with students, it is the equivalent of having students move content with a bulldozer. Rote memorizing would be like moving academic content with a shovel. They are moving that much more educational content and not even breaking a sweat in the process. The student can learn much more information, and it takes less cognitive energy. When we teach using these different brain techniques, students will build confidence in their learning because they retain the information. It can help students transition from thinking they are dumb to knowing that they can learn complex content. The more they learn, the stronger their brain gets.

Chapter 10: Packing In The Mountains

PACKING IN THE MOUNTAINS

Quite a switch, I know, to go from talking about the brain back to talking about horses. It is a pairing between sweet and salty. Too much of one thing can be overbearing, but if we can find a complementary balance, it can enhance the experience.

After the Christian horse camp had closed down, I was back to being jobless for the summer. I was driving back from a branding one weekend when I got a call. It was a gall explaining that one of the kids I had worked with at the summer camp was applying for a job with her as a dude wrangler. This term might be new to you. A dude wrangler is the person who gets the horses ready for the guests to get on. Then, we take them for a ride and, to the best of our ability, ensure they get home safely! Often, the term dude wrangler will get shortened to wrangler. I explained to the gal on the phone what the employee's ability was. The gal on the phone paused and then asked if I wanted the job. I was not expecting that. I told her I could only answer her once I saw the horses. In the dude business, we inevitably end up with old and sore horses, but they are still good enough to take people for a trail ride. I understand that an outfit must use sore horses, but my concern is how they are taken care of. Are they in good flesh? That is how we explain that the horses have been fed well and cared for.

I explained to the gal on the phone that I had been branding all weekend. I was dirty, stinky, and lacking sleep. I had my horse in the trailer, but if she were okay with that, I would show up and check things out! She agreed and looked forward to meeting me.

I showed up just as advertised with my manual truck and horse in the horse trailer. I backed it into a little hole on the first try, and the kindest gal met me to shake my hand and introduce herself. We talked for a little bit, but it was probably hours. It was one of those conversations that went so easily you lost track of time. Their horses were in good flesh, and we had the same ideas on accomplishing this kind of work. She offered me a job, and I took it.

I started the following weekend; I saddled my horse and many others that morning. When you have been around the business long enough, you will come across people who can talk but don't have the walk. By the time I saddled my first horse, and she saddled her first horse, there was no doubt that what we advertised about ourselves was the truth.

I rode two or three trips, with her following along. This place where we do the dude rides is in the trees and has trails that crisscross every way. I am a preferred flat lander, sagebrush country guy. When she asked if I was ready to take a group out? I said, "Yes, I think I can figure it out!" I can read tracks well enough. I will follow the tracks around this park, and I should be good! I hoped my ability to read tracks would compensate for my lack of knowing where I was in the trees. Well, away I went with this group, chatting and having a good time! When I came across the first set of options, I read the tracks, and away we went, not a problem. The guest probably had no idea that I didn't know where I was. After another couple of switches in the trail, I was doing good, building up some confidence and smiling inside a bit for being able to cheat my way through. Well, what I didn't know was that my boss took out another group. She took a different path and, mid-way through, crossed the tracks. When I got to the spot where the tracks got crossed, I didn't know where to go! Based on my limited sense of direction, I took a guess, which was stifled by the trees, and it turned out wrong. Well, I returned to camp about thirty minutes later than expected. My boss was not worried, but we did have a good laugh when I explained my approach.

Another brand-new thing to me with this outfit was that they sold timed rides. So, my boss sold a thirty-minute ride, an hour ride, an hour and a half and longer if they wanted. I was used to riding a trail. So, I was not used to watching the time. In all honesty, I still have no use for time. If I could get up when I awake, eat when I'm hungry, and go to bed when I am tired, I would be completely okay with getting rid of clocks altogether. Slowly but surely, I learned the trails well enough to get around. I always enjoyed taking the dudes out and working the cabin. I got to meet some incredible people! I could tune out and ride my circle if they were not interesting people to talk to. Then, you get back and get a chance at another group.

Well, it took little time and my boss saw my potential in getting me packing. She asked if I knew how to pack. I explained that I had little experience but not much. I told her I was good with a mule but willing to learn anything and everything else. They did a great job teaching me, and by the end of the first summer, I was packing some loads by myself. I knew just enough to be dangerous, as the old saying goes!

We were soon doing overnight trips and becoming quite the team. At that time, I was still bouncing between day rides and overnight trips. This next story takes place at the cabin where we did day rides.

I had an older guy and his daughter-in-law on this trip. Usually, when I hear you have an older couple, I cringe a bit because they are generally not in good enough physical shape to enjoy the ride. Many think riding a horse is as simple as sitting on a rocking chair and going for a joy ride. For most people, the novelty wears off in about thirty minutes, and then they realize that riding a horse requires real work. Anyway, I took them on the ride, and I had developed a rote that would allow me to give people shortcuts back home. I would always provide them with a choice. I would ask how they felt and whether they wanted the ride to be longer or shorter. He replied that it was a great ride, but he had seen more wildlife in his backyard in Arizona. I explained if we went the longer way, we might have a chance to see some elk! They were excited, and he was in good enough shape to keep riding, so we went in that direction. As we approached the corner, a cow elk was lying in the meadow. They were excited and started taking pictures. Just then, she gave a big ol stretch, much like a dog would. Then she put her head down and charged me. It caught me by surprise, and my instincts kicked in, and I ran my horse at her. She gave up the bluff right at the last second. I started hollering at her, and she bumped off, then lined me up and charged again. I realized she wasn't going to give up easily. In between the charges, I told the guest to ride past and get to a safe place and that I would be there as soon as possible. She charged me about six more times. I thought she wanted to crawl in the saddle with me. I finally got past her. Looking back, I am sure she had a baby in the brush somewhere. It was the first time that I experienced a wild animal that wouldn't just scare off. The guests were all good. I kept them safe, and they appreciated it. I gained more respect for the animals when I got close enough to have their snot flung on me. The elk are powerful animals, and hell hath no fury like a pissed-off mother.

This next story takes place a couple of summers after the first summer. I had gotten to the point where I could pack my own loads, take a string of mules, and get almost any job done. Before this story, I had bumped two bears around our mountain camp. You usually get to see a black or brown flash as they go crashing away. Those kinds of sightings are enjoyable. Our horses are so used to being around them that they tend not to spook much.

I was making a feed run. These are my favorite, in all honesty, because feed is easy to pack. Feed is easy to pack because the loads don't usually try to spin. After all, you are packing a pre-measured equal weight on both sides. For those who do not know, the big goal with packing is to get your loads weighing the same on both sides. Having equal weights is quickly done at home with a scale but is more difficult when you are at the parking lot packing or picking up a drop camp.

Anyway, I was three hours into the trip. I had a string of five or six mules, and the trip was going well. I was on the last home stretch before camp and bumped into a bear. The only difference was this time, he didn't go running off completely. He ran a little, stopped, sat on his hind end, and looked at me and the pack string. I started hollering to scare him off, but that didn't work. He returned to his walking position and started moving towards me and the pack string. I had my pistol drawn and ready to go when this thought flashed through my head: if I shoot my gun, I am liable to be in the middle of a runaway, horse, and string of mules in the woods. I have never shied away from a bucking horse or a runaway, but you can be the best rider and still get in a bad wreck when surrounded by so many trees. If that runaway takes a trip under a branch that they can make but you can't, well, this can be detrimental to your health.

Luckily, I had to cross a creek before camp. As I did, that bear lost interest and must have decided what he smelled was not worth getting wet. When you face off with a wild animal, and it does not scare the animal away, it will make you respect Mother Nature a little bit more. In this life, when you grow up in the city, unknowingly, you acquire this perception that the human being is at the top of the animal hierarchy. People think that they can control Mother Nature. Moments like that remind me of how little I am. Mother Nature can be ruthless and malicious, and that bear has no concept of the fact that he might be put to death if he murders a human. He has no ideas of consequences or morality. His choices are governed by hunger, water, safety, and what he must do to stay alive in the moment. You can be the most intelligent, well-spoken, wealthiest, and most humane person, and you have no chance of talking that bear out of an attack.

Now, onto another story. I had one trip with a bunch of gals. I had two mules, and the loads were packed in without problems. We were close to the heartbeat number that the Wilderness would allow. To understand this, we are set to a 12-heartbeat limit. So, you and your horse would be two heartbeats. With the group and their horses, the group was at 11 heartbeats. So, I had to camp further away and run back and forth to take care of both stock sets, get fed, and entertain the group. They were an entertaining group of gals.

So, we were coming to the end of the trip. The gals put their pile of stuff on a canvas tarp and left it there for me to pick up. My boss and the group headed out ahead of me because we couldn't have the groups together because of the heartbeat rule. So, I get there and start packing my loads for my two mules. In the packing industry, we have loads called marsh mellow loads. A marshmallow load is big and puffy. I got my loads set, and down the trail I went. I had Blondie at the end. Blondie was one of my favorite mules; in his younger days, he was known for taking advantage of people if they did not know what they were doing. He and I got along well enough, but he was one of those mules you had to be careful around him. He also had a pretty round-back. So, if you didn't get your loads just right, they tended to lean one way, and if you weren't careful, they would slip under him. If that happened, it could be a nasty wreck to get out of, especially with a sensitive mule. I came off the first section, and his load listed or leaned slightly. I wanted to fix it before it became a big problem. My problem was that I didn't have a good tree to tie to. I had one for my horse, but that was it. The trail was narrow, and I didn't want to slip my load. So, I tied my horse to the tree and tied my lead mule to my saddle like I had seen my boss do many times. Just as I popped my crow's foot, the lead mule decided to walk ahead of my horse. He pulled the lead rope through the horn and ran off. The lead mule was dragging the mule I was trying to fix the load on. Usually, the breakaway would break, and I would have lost only one mule, but it didn't on that trip. I hopped on my horse, chasing them at a long trot, hoping to find a spot to get around them. As they ran down the trail, they were losing their loads everywhere. It looked like a yard sale all down the trail. I could never get past and stop them, but luckily, they ran into the group. We gathered them back up, and the boss helped me square them away. Over a mile, I had to carry loads back to where I could get the mules packed up again. After that, down the trail, we went.

That was something that my boss appreciated about me. Mistakes happen, but when they do, you work hard to fix them. I didn't blame anything; animals will be animals, and the best packers will all have stories of when everything went wrong.

The next day, I had another long trip with heavy loads. I took that mule in with me and packed him heavy that day. I told my friend you might be so mad at a mule that you want to give him the thumping that he deserves, but that won't get you anywhere with a mule. You have to punish a mule the mule way, and after packing those heavy loads the next day, he knew that he had messed up.

Those years working for that outfit allowed me to get to know people from all over the world. Some-times, it would be a trip with a couple or a father and daughter who saved for a long time to afford the trip. Others were so wealthy they could write a check for the entire outfit. But being in the woods is a great equalizer. It takes them only a short time to determine that their safety depends on our knowledge of the woods and horses. The beauty of that is that it boils down to being human beings. I have had conversations about the depth of the morality and issues of providing humans with a super brain pill. That pill could improve intellectual capability to the point of being able to dive into the depths of creativity and ingenuity to be able to solve global issues.

On the other hand, I have had conversations about horses, family, love, and many other issues. I have made friends along the way and gained experiences that I will never forget. I had bosses who truly appreciated the work and effort I put into the job. I also had bosses who never asked me to do something they would not be willing to do. The memories I created while working for them could fill volumes. The challenge was not to be able to write a book about all the great times but the challenge was to keep the book under a thousand pages. To all the guests I got to work with and my bosses for those great years, I want to say thank you.

Chapter 11: Learning About Teaching By Teaching

LEARNING ABOUT TEACHING BY TEACHING

I once had a professor who said that if you are willing to learn from your students, they will learn from you. The advice he gave me has so many implications throughout academia. In the same sense I discussed earlier, if you want to get great at throwing a football, you have to throw a football a lot. If you're going to get great at teaching, you have to teach a lot. The hard fact of it is that you are going to make a lot of mistakes. You will even make more mistakes at the beginning. Making mistakes is part of the neurological process of learning. If you are making mistakes, it is because you are putting yourself out there and taking a chance. The essential things that I have found as a teacher are that you have a heart that genuinely cares for the students and their success, an attitude that you can find the answer if you do not know the answer, the resilience to work together until you get it and know that they will get better as a student. If you approach each day with those essentials, have confidence that you will improve as a teacher.

If you struggle with classroom management, you might have to read several books, go onto YouTube to watch lectures on behavioral psychology or find a teacher who does a great job at classroom management to learn what to do better. If you spend years practicing to get better, you will, but if you spend years practicing the same things, you will continue to get the same problems.

One of the most challenging pills for a teacher to swallow is it isn't the student's fault. If you come home and continuously blame your tough day on the group of students that you have, you are missing it! That might mean you need to take a giant step back and ask yourself, what am I doing that is causing them to act this way? I see this many times in the horse world. How the person rides can cause the horse to flip its head with bit pressure, and for some reason, every horse they buy starts flipping its head to bit pressure after a month or so of riding. I tell these people there is nothing wrong with your horse. The problem is you! That is hard for some people to undertake, but the beauty is that you can change what you are doing, so you can get a different result if you are willing to do the work. If you keep doing what you have always done, you will keep getting what you have always gotten.

I just recently had a parent email me about a student. He is doing well in my class and another class. First, I told the parent there was nothing wrong with their child. He does well when he knows that his teacher truly cares about him as a person. From there, we can build students up! It may take some digging, but one of the ideas I hold to help with this is to find out why this student is in my class and what I can do to help them improve. Is it because there is something that I need to teach them? Or I need to learn from them. When things get tough, some students can bring humor to the room. Some students might act as thermometers for the class. Every student has a purpose for being in class, and it is your job as the teacher to find that purpose.

I started out giving tests that would take three days to complete. At the time, students would have to take these extensive standardized tests at the end of the year. So, I thought, like athletics, let's try to train harder than the state test. You will prepare for twenty rounds if you are a boxer and have a ten-round fight. As an athlete, I understood this idea of over-training. That way, when it is game day, the game is easy. I tried applying this cognitively. My only problem was I forgot about incremental training. We have to increase the rigor and the training until game day slowly. At the time, I understood the hard work it would take, but I needed to learn how fragile a student's confidence can be.

Another of my innocent misconceptions was that if I gave students four different problems on the same topic, I could better identify where the student was making the conceptual mistake. It did help me to identify the students' misconceptions. But, being honest with myself, it got many of my students not wanting to be in my class as well. They dreaded the hour when I would shove math past saturation into their minds. My saving grace was that the students knew I cared about them and wanted them to be successful.

Another great way to learn from your students is by giving them student evaluation reflections. Student evaluations are a great tool to improve your teaching. Be warned that the students can be brutally honest.

So, you have to hear what they say, but you cannot be offended by what they say. Otherwise, the next time you ask for honest feedback, they will not be willing to do so. In the reflections, try to pull at least one thing that you can change and do it. Being willing to change shows the students that you care about what they say. Later in my career, this practice started to die off when students said, " Don't change anything. You're doing a great job!" Again, I am not saying that to pat myself on the back. It is to pat the process on the back. If you learn from each group of students, they will help you to become a better teacher. I want to be the most outstanding teacher possible to help the most significant number of students. Ultimately, it is never about me but always about the student. Remember, it is the student's education. Don't try to take that from them.

Listen to your student's story! Many times, you do not even have to give any advice. You have to listen and care. I had yet to learn about the poverty and struggles that many of our students face in this district. One time, I did a survey asking students about their home lives. I had two students out of 120 who said everything was great, and they had two parents at home who loved them. Now understand that we, as human beings, tend to fixate on the problems in our lives, not the great things happening. We all have struggles, and that includes our students. Later in my career, when new teachers or principals ask what they need to know about the students, I will tell them the difficulties our students tell us about are probably accurate. When a student tells you that they were not able to do their homework because mom's druggy boyfriend was in a rage last night, and they spent the whole night hiding in the closet, that is probably true. It might be a miracle that many of our students make it to school daily. When that student puts their head down to sleep in class, it might be because they listened to their baby sibling cry all night. We are all human beings, and if our basic needs are unmet, we will not have the brain power to think about mathematics or other academic subjects. If a student is thinking about food or water, where they might sleep that night, if they will have warm enough clothes for the next day, or why their parents were fighting, they will be entirely consumed by these thoughts of survival.

It amazes me that we can help these students learn. They might not be able to learn on the daily. At times, their plate might be so heavy that it is all they can carry, but think of it this way: would it be better if they learned three days out of the week or if they didn't learn any of the days? I ask this because if you get them in trouble for sleeping in class and do not understand that they are exhausted, they will think you do not care about them. They will completely tune you out because, in all honesty, you do not even care about their basic needs, so why would they give you the little brain power that they might have left? You can gain much more ground with the kids if you ask them why they are so tired and listen to them. Whatever the reason, be willing to listen. You might be surprised by what they are willing to tell you.

Be a leader, not a dictator. Whenever you can show the kids what to do, it will be way better than just telling them what to do. Model the behaviors you want students to perform. So, if you mess up, apologize when you're wrong. Being a leader can be as simple as picking up garbage and scraps off the floor before I ask students to do it. If you want students to put their cell phones away during instruction, then put your cell phone away during instruction. If you want students to use repeated addition when they do not know the answer to a multiplication problem, you should occasionally use repeated addition to figure out multiplication. I will even do the assignments with the students as well. I might have a project where they are turning a formula into a picture, and I will give it a go myself. Doing the assignment can also be an excellent tool for pacing. You should finish first, so give them the extra time to complete the assignment. Also, avoid getting so wrapped up in what you're doing that you forget to walk around the class and check in on what the students are doing.

I have had hard times in my personal life. I have had loved ones pass away. I will tell my students I am here, but I am struggling. I will then explain to an appropriate level why I am having a tough time, and being able to model what to do when you are having social and emotional issues demonstrates to the students that I am a human just like them. Students will be able to relate better to you, and you will encourage the students to be empathetic. Students will often be extra kind because they care so much about you. It boils down to two simple rules: never tell the students to do something you are unwilling to do and don't be a hypocrite.

Be kind to your colleagues, but only have one true work friend. I started out being friends with a great group of teachers. We all got hired around the same time. They were great support through learning how to be a teacher. The more people you are friends with at work, if you overshare about your personal life, they can use that information against you. As you pick your work friend, notice who the kids like and respect. Students will associate you with their coolness if you hang around that person. Also, hanging around that person will teach you the things that they do that students respect. You will share ideas and realize their core beliefs, allowing you to build rapport with your students. You can't be them, but you can adapt their techniques to work for you. Teaching is challenging. You will need someone in the profession that you can honestly share what is going on. If they are a good work friend, they will not judge but offer suggestions to help or give you a different perspective.

Be private with the details you share with your colleagues. The less they know about you, the better. The wise person is the one who listens, not the one who talks. Sharing a little about yourself will reduce your stress at the workplace, but it might increase the rumors. Just remember, if they are talking about you, it might be because they do not understand what you are doing. Or, your colleagues might be jealous of the relationships you have with students. Keep business at work and your life at home as much as you can. At times, I have gone into character to help myself with this. You can still be authentic, but you don't have to say everything that comes to your mind.

Teachers love to tell other teachers what to do. They think they can teach you too. The help the other teachers have to offer is excellent if they are a better teacher than you are, but if they are not a better teacher, be careful to avoid consuming the poison they have to offer.

Each group of students, from year to year, will teach you something new. Their motivations will change. How you must reach them will change. What they find funny will change. What they already know will change. A healthy society is changing, growing, and adapting to what it needs to be, and the classroom is no different. Never quite trying and never quite caring! If you go to work with a positive attitude, students will pick that up and understand that you enjoy being there. Learning these things has helped me reach more students and hopefully will help you, too!

Chapter 12: Day Working

DAY WORKING

Day working is some of the best cowboy work there is to do. When I became a teacher, I stopped being invited to some brandings around my area. I asked a buddy how this was, and he explained it was because I wasn't a cowboy. That hurt a bit, but I have since made peace with it. It was true my occupation was not a cowboy, but I love to be around it. I love working with the horses. I love working with the cows. I love every aspect of cowboying. I decided to provide a more stable income for my family. I wanted their financial well-being independent of cattle, diesel, and feed prices.

Cowboys define day-working by only being hired from day to day. A ranch barely squeaks by financially. To make it work, most ranches are understaffed, not overstaffed. One cowboy may be on the payroll, and twenty hoof rots pop up simultaneously! Having so many animals getting sick at the same time might be too much work for one cowboy to get done in a timely fashion. So, the rancher might hire a day-working cowboy to come and help rope all the animals because a two-person doctor is easier than a one-person doctor.

And this is where I smile because day work is perfect for me. I can rope and handle cattle well enough to help most ranches get any job done. Working for many different outfits also allows me to see how different outfits do things. The best part is I don't have to irrigate or drive a tractor. Don't get me wrong, I understand the necessity of irrigating and building fences. But I prefer to work cattle horseback.

Another significant aspect of day working is you always get to see new country. When we get to cowboy, we can often work in some of the most beautiful places. Usually, the cowboys who work in the same area day after day lose sight of the beauty they are surrounded by. It is also why I do not want to train horses full-time. I wanted my passion to retain its luster by not overindulging in it. I have traveled to many places to enjoy the beauty and then move on before the beauty starts to fade.

Also, everyone trains their cattle differently. Each rancher will argue why one way is better than another. The property you run your cows on can significantly dictate how you must train them. For example, if you have cattle on irrigated smaller pastures, low-stress handling and walking the cattle from pasture to pasture makes sense. On the contrary, if you have cattle on a vast pasture, gathering one pasture would take a whole day if everything walked from one end to the other. On these giant pastures, we ride to the back part of the pasture and bust the pastures. To bust a pasture, you get whooping and hollering and ride a big circle around the outside edge of the pasture. The idea is that the cattle will run out of all the rock formations and brush. Also, when the cattle start trotting out, it will signal to other cattle it's time to get a move on. This technique helps in the country where you can't easily ride every step of it. Believe it or not, cattle can get into places a good cowboy would prefer not to ride. I have seen calves jump off 8-foot cap rock, land going down a hill, and never miss a step in the process.

A big part of life is figuring out what you enjoy doing and setting your life to do those things. Keep your passions like your favorite savory treat. If you try to live on that treat alone, you will quickly learn that it is not enough to sustain yourself. Save your treat for when you genuinely need a recharge or to bribe yourself to do something you do not want to do.

Also, day work has allowed me to form some of my best relationships. One outfit that I have worked for the boss and his family has become a part of my family. I have watched his kids grow from youngsters to fine young adults. We have gained a particular bond from when you go through challenges from a hard day's work, then ride in the pickup together, discuss what you did right, and what you could do better next time. Our conversations often dive deep into life's complexities and what we must do to maintain healthy relationships. We cry on each other's shoulders when times are tough and celebrate when times are good. Often, we are each other's unbiased view of where we are at. We love each other enough to tell the other person when we agree or disagree. They understand you because they have lived that life, and you know them from the countless hours you have worked with them. It has allowed me to marvel at God's glory and fellowship with a brother.

Most importantly, I get to talk about the things that I love to talk about, and they get to do the same as well. I can't help but smile thinking about all the different things we have chatted about over the years. If the truck could have recorded what we said, we probably would be able to solve all the world's problems. A true friend who only wants to build you up, and you want to do the same for them. You share meals, time, laughs, prayers, and love together.

Another part of the day working is branding season. I have always said branding is what I live for. If I had a string of horses, a good saddle, enough ropes, and had to live out of a bedroll, I would live that way if I could continuously brand all year round. Traveling from ranch to ranch to help get this job done is rewarding. Traveling to a bunch of different ranches also provides more opportunities to trade. Trading is a favorite pastime of a lot of cowboys. You might end up with a beautiful piece of gear, but it doesn't work for you, so you trade it for something that might fit you or your string better. If you make something, this is a great way to trade into something you want. I enjoy braiding, so I make some bosals, reins, lead ropes, mecates, halters, etc. I might trade a handful of hondas (rawhide braded into a loop that goes onto the end of rope) something a cowboy needs because he has worn his last one out, for a mecate that he has an extra of. More traveling means more opportunities to trade.

Now for a day-working story. One branding story I got to tell happened to a good buddy of mine. To understand completely, I must explain where his horsemanship and roping started. He had been around horses most of his life growing up. If I were to make a guess, like many people who grow up around horses, that does not mean they grew up around excellent horsemanship. That being said, that does not mean that he can't recognize fine horsemanship. He started roping later in his life after retirement. Amazingly, he lived with that dream for as long as he did, and when his life finally allowed him to explore it, he did. I had helped him learn how to train his horse, and he really enjoyed learning more and would always practice as much as he could. I helped with his roping, and we got him to make a few catches in the branding pen. It was fantastic to be a part of that process with him and see him going from zero to being able to catch something. It is like watching your kid make their first basket. We are all proud of the growth that he made.

Now, the branding pen can also be dangerous. There are calves, horses, sharp objects, mean momma cows, and endless possibilities of things going wrong. Our job as a more experienced hand is to help avoid as many wrecks as possible. This buddy of mine had thrown a loop and had caught a calf. Now, you must understand my boss's calves are not light. These calves come off the range, and they know how to survive. They are tough young adults, often weighing more than a strong man, anywhere between 200 and 300 pounds. So, he had the calf caught, and he had dropped a few coils when he threw his loop, and when he pulled his slack up, the coils had wrapped around his leg. He was excited for the catch, and he went to his dally. It was one of those moments that happened only by the grace of God. I barely even remember what had happened, but I had pulled my knife and cut his rope before his leg was pulled out of the socket from a three-hundred-pound calf and a 1,300-pound horse. Seeing me coming, he said, "I am fine, don't worry about it." I responded, "No, you're not." As I cut his rope. After the adrenaline had worn off from catching the calf and almost getting caught in a bad wreck, he thanked me for what I did. The story's moral is that no matter how young or old a person is in the trap, we cowboys do our best to protect everyone. Although expensive, a cut rope is better than a hurt buddy. That is part of that camaraderie built when you work a dangerous job, day working, and branding.

At times, there are things that you can do to help a buddy, and at other times, there is nothing you can do to help. One of the traditions in the branding pen is if you rope a cow, you have to ride it. This rule also applies to renegade steers or bulls. Renegades are animals that have somehow avoided the two main gathers, either branding season or fall gathering. We had one of these yearling bulls in the pen that needed to be branded and castrated. Some other cowboys got the animal roped, and I was on the ground helping get the ropes set. Working with these heavy and older animals is a dangerous job because of the sheer weight and strength of the animals. If they flop their head on top of your foot, they can easily break your toes or foot. Even though I had not accidentally roped this animal, the consensus was that I should ride this bull. Not wanting to let the rest of the cowboys down, I accepted this challenge. After castration of a mostly grown animal, they tend to be pretty mad when they first get up. Knowing that the animal can get up mad after castration was part of my calculated plan. I outweighed the risks and figured that being on his back was the safest place. Since I was sitting on the animal lying down, my boss kindly worked on getting the animal up. The first and safest approach is to twist the animal's tail. Twisting his tail was not working. He then worked on re-positioning the animal's head. Switching the steer's head worked well, and the animal started to get up. When he got up, I was now riding the animal, and my boss was the focus of rage for this new adult steer. I picked the best spot to bail, throwing my leg over to the back while the animal ran my boss down. The steer gave him a little bump with his head for good measures. No one was hurt, so it continues to be a story we tell with a good smile and humor. Sometime later, I put these words together, "You can lead a bull to town by the whiskers as long as you stay one step ahead of him!" My poor boss didn't even make it as far as the other end of the branding pen, but I can assure you he was applying the maximum amount of effort to get away, and it is incredible how much effort you can find when you are running for your life.

Chapter 13: How It Might Work In The Classroom

HOW IT MIGHT WORK IN THE CLASSROOM

How you can teach your classroom will depend on your principal and what they think of you. If your principal likes you, then teaching life is easy, and you can do whatever you want within the realm of professional practice. Things can be much more complicated if the principal does not like you, but doing what is best for the students is still possible.

When a principal does not like you, your whole goal is to disappear as much as possible. It would help if you put on a show when they are around. Acting sounds like a horrible thing to say, but when they are around, show them what they want to see. Whatever your evaluation system is, find a book on it and read it. Know it better than your principal because that is how they will try to get you. To win, you have to have it so clearly documented that you can hand your evidence over to anyone else, and they can look at it and tell the principal that they are wrong. Once you have shown the principal a handful of times that you are doing what they want you to do, you can do the right thing for the students all the other times they are not around. Putting on a show seems slightly deceitful, but if a principal is out to get you, they are not playing the game by the rules. They should be encouraging you and building you up. That being said, not all principals play ethically.

One of the things that I do that makes many teachers and principals mad is that all my students get the letter grade of an A in the first trimester. Teach every student how to be successful in your class. You can then gradually release more responsibility for the next trimesters to follow. I start my students with an A because if you care for them and show them what they need to do to get an A, they are likelier to keep doing the correct things when they have more choice over their academics. If they get an F, then they will quit trying to learn. So, let's keep the kids trying and improving. With winter here, while I write this, I can't help but think of education as a survival hike in the snow. The company you keep can significantly depend on your success. When the going gets tough, do you want the person with you who is telling you that you can do this or the person who is telling you that you can't accomplish the task? Do you want the person willing to carry your pack when the snow gets deep or the person who is like you didn't make it far enough fast enough, so you failed? As a teacher, I believe we have to encourage our students every step. Show them that they can do it, and if they can't accomplish it on their own, you will be there to help them. You will help carry their load as long as they keep stepping forward.

The problem with encouraging kids by showing them they earned an A will also upset many teachers and some principals. Students won't respect teachers who try to force them into learning by punishing them with bad grades. So, ensure you have a system to show teachers and principals that students are learning at high levels. For me, I had an online standardized test.

If you are a decent teacher, you will find a way to get students to be successful on the test. Teach to the test. Most people will not say that, but they will quickly judge your teaching if students do not do well on standardized tests. I have one test my students only care a little about. The students tend to guess on this test and not try their best. Students do not try on the test because of public perception of the test. So, I have one test that they do not do well on and another test that they do well on. When you have two tests, one that they score high on and one that they score low on, it creates confusion with the administration and other teachers. If you play it correctly, you can use that confusion to your benefit.

Other teachers will try to argue that because students get an A, your class lacks rigor. The test I would use, I managed to get all but four students above grade level. Some students scored three to four grade levels above their grade. Of the four students who did not score above grade level, two were at grade level and previously were not, and the other two students improved by more than two grade levels in one year. Make sure to have evidence like that in your back pocket. If they attack you, that is okay, but I will not let people attack the hard work and effort that my students put in.

A principal accused me of not having enough rigor in my class. I politely asked him to define what he thought rigor meant. He tried saying that he thought rigor provided enough repetitions for students to remember it. So, I exclaimed, "Like rote memorization?" He didn't want to compare it to that. If you recall from the section on the brain, rote memorization is the least efficient way to memorize and learn something. It requires the most time and brain energy to accomplish it. I then asked the principal if running an eight-minute mile would be rigorous for him. He said that it would be rigorous for him. I told him that it would be easy for me. That is the challenging piece of rigor. You can only define it for an individual. You have to know the individual well enough to know their level of rigor. Most importantly, you must have a strong relationship with the students to push them into a level of rigor. I believe in rigor, but you should start slowly and build into it. Show the students they can accomplish level one before you ask them to attempt level two.

Another way you can pull off getting students good grades is by giving them credit for the effort that they put into it. Yes, this can be explained as a participation grade in some ways, although that can put a sour taste in some people's mouths. Rewarding effort is an excellent academic method, but better athletic practices might exist. I agree that in life, there are times when you will win and times when you will lose. The real question, in academics, is, do you want kids to lose? If you don't, then by all means, find a way for them to win. The way I explain it is no child left behind and no problem left behind. If a student does not know how to solve a problem, work with them until they can. Even better yet, getting another student to work with them until they get it will help both students. Students helping each other is way more powerful than the teacher helping the student because you create an environment where the only way to succeed is by working together.

Also, cognitively, one of the best ways to learn something is by teaching it. So, both students gain even more by working together. In the real world, the boss has to show his employees that he is willing and can do all the jobs, but they have to delegate the work to place their effort into running the business. Your role as a teacher is the same as being a boss for a company.

My goal as a teacher is to bring the whole group together and raise them higher academically. In college, I had to create my teaching philosophy. My teacher philosophy is I want the last to become first and the first to become better. So, teachers often need help with what to do with their high-performing students to keep them engaged and challenged. Giving them further mathematics that their classmates are not ready for only creates a competitive environment where the only way to win is by others losing. We do not want that. So, to keep them engaged with what we are learning, I suggest they create an example problem for their classmates. Sometimes, they create a challenging math problem but allow all students to go through the struggle. Afterward, discuss how they could re-write the problem to make it work better. The students that get the content quickly have them become the student teachers and go around and help their classmates. Make sure it is not always the same students that are the student teachers. We do not want to create an environment where some students think they are better than others.

Sometimes, I purposely show a student who might struggle a little trick to make the math easier. Then, I will have them show their class. Giving them credit for the idea can boost their confidence and show the class that everyone's ideas are essential to building the learning community. In some units, I will have four student teachers. I will teach the four students the quick lesson and then have them teach a small group.

Do not overspread yourself. If you do, you will do nothing tremendous and everything average. Use your best energy to do the best things. When you master one thing, then master another. Mastering something before you move on to learning the next thing can apply to your home and work life.

When the administration asks you if you can volunteer for something, I will start by asking when they need an answer. Creating a break from when the person asks the question until you answer does a few things. It shows that you are wise and will contemplate where you spend your time. Also, the administration is often looking for quick yeses and will find them from someone else before you can answer, thus relieving you from the duty. I have usually recommended to teachers that they tell the principal that you would like to check with your spouse before you make a decision. You want to avoid getting involved in something that will not pay and cost you time and energy. That sounds selfish, but you need to protect your time. Do not work for free. Getting you to work for free is stealing from you. We need compensation for our time. All too often, teachers feel that to find favor amongst the administration, they must do everything they ask of them. When exploited, it is much easier to use you the next time. My rule is that if it directly helps a student, I have no problem helping. If it is one of those meetings where a lot is said, but nobody accomplishes anything, I avoid those at all costs. Volunteering less also helps to build a robust and independent persona. Keeping a little distance from work will help you maintain your independence.

Not saying yes always will also prevent your peers from thinking you are a teacher's pet or a snitch. Not being in the administration's pocket is essential because they will likely trust you with information. The more information you have, the better your chances are to survive politically. Always receive information and seldom share information. If you share some information, never attach what you have heard to someone. As much as it sucks to say but to some degree, your job is a chess match. Play the moves that will best protect yourself, and play the moves that will help you advance the most. I have seen the best teachers and people get consumed by their peers. It does not matter how awesome you are. Someone will dislike you, and someone will think you are doing your job wrong.

On a similar note, find something you can get paid for that gets you involved with the students outside of class. For myself, that was coaching. It might be coaching, running the concession stand, knowledge bowl coach, FFA advisor, or any other activity you can get paid to do. Being involved with an activity outside the general school day will help your reputation with the students grow. Students view us teachers as these things that never leave the classroom. Being involved in other activities shows your students that you are an actual human and are interested in different things besides the school subject you teach. It will also show the students that you invest in the school. Being around students outside class is also a great way to show your sense of humor. Keep your humor light, never about a person, and always appropriate. I enjoy pointing out the irony as part of my sense of humor. I also will refer to literature or something popular that is going on. Keep it light and funny, but this also helps you build enjoyability in class and relationships. Everyone enjoys a good laugh. Just make sure that it is never laughing at a person.

Another great thing to remember as you become a teacher is that it will not always be perfect. There will be more imperfect times in teaching than ideal times, which is okay! Students will have bad days, and you will have bad days, which is just part of being human. If you have built a classroom atmosphere of respect and are honest with your students, this can go a long way.

One time, after three or four years of teaching, we unexpectedly lost a student. We returned from Thanksgiving break, and the principal brought us into the library. He informed us that one of our students had passed away. He had underlying medical issues that his family knew about, but, as his teacher, I had no idea. It was one of those moments that hurt me deep inside. I have always said you can do anything to me, but don't mess with my kids. The administration informed us to move on because our kids need that. I could not disagree more. I believe that we need to teach kids about the grieving process and different coping mechanisms that might help them healthily deal with grief.

I told my students that when my grandpa passed away, I had a period of extreme anger. I didn't realize at the time that anger is part of the way that I mourn. I explained to them that they might feel feelings that don't make sense, which is okay. Weeks later, I heard a song that reminded me of that exceptional student, and I started that day a wreck. I stood before my class and told them about hearing that song and how it affected me. I told them that I was having difficulty processing those emotions and would need their help. I needed them to take it easy on me that day. The crazy part about it is they did. They understood, and they also learned a valuable lesson. I am human, and so are they. It is okay to tell people when you are not feeling okay. It is better than trying to hold it in.

Similarly, I was helping tutor a young man with a brain injury. I heard about him out of district and was excited to be his mentor. Not only has this young man suffered a brain injury, but he also had a tough home life. At the time, his teacher gave him the you need to be happy and thankful speech to him. I had to tell her that was not what he needed to hear. Not everything is fairy tales and rainbows. There will be tough times in your life, and you might be in one of those tough times right now. I will not tell you that you need to think happy thoughts, which will make it all better. That is great, but it differs from what will help in the long run.

Often, these suffering people know how to solve their problems. I asked, "When you get overwhelmed, how can you help yourself feel better?" He jokingly said, "Go outside and smoke a cigarette." I said, "Nice try, buddy. You have to come up with something that is making you better, not harming you!" He then told me how he was really into native survival. He told me how it felt like all his other troubles, and he could set them aside while learning about native survival. That is great. That is the good stuff. He knew what he needed to do. He did not need to be treated like a baby. He was a young man and needed to be treated like a young man. He just needed someone to care about him and listen. Many times, that is enough to help them solve their problems. Be genuine and honest with students. I believe they will appreciate and respect that.

Chapter 14: How To Play The School Game

HOW TO PLAY THE SCHOOL GAME

Play it in any way that allows you to win. I had a roommate who once said, "Beg, borrow, cheat, or steal your way through college; get it done however you have to get it done." I try to promote a more ethical means of accomplishing academics, but at the end of the day, the most crucial part is completing it. Most importantly, deciding how you want to run the race before you start would be best.

One thing I enjoy watching on YouTube is people hiking the Pacific Crest Trail. Interestingly, everyone writes rules on how they want to accomplish the trial. Some people are strict and believe that even if there is a closure on the trail due to fires or something else, they have to walk around the detour. Others are less strict with themselves, and if they have to stick their thumb out and catch a ride to the next section of the trail, they will. With school, know what you want to get out of it and ensure you get that out of it. I am a firm believer that it is your education. If you have a question, raise your hand and ask it. Raising your hand to ask a question seems simple, but so many students could learn so much more of the content if they would engage in it and ask the questions that they have.

One of the most significant techniques for learning the material is to try and find a way to connect the new material to something you already know a lot about. Cognitively, you are attaching the latest information to something you already know. Connecting the new information helps you because you can easily recall what you already know, which will instantly activate the recent memory. Another way of understanding how connecting new information to old ideas is like a filing cabinet. A filling cabinet allows you to store the newly learned information in a place you can return and find.

My next big tip is to break your sessions into several small study times. Studying for a test will help you more if you spend three different times studying for ten minutes than if you try to study one time for an hour. You can test how long your brain can pay attention to one task. The easy test for this is to start a timer and start reading. Once you realize or notice that you are thinking about something other than what you are reading, hit stop. You can try this a couple of times. As you repeat this test, you can determine a good average. When you study, set a timer for how much time you can easily pay attention. For each session, you should only study for that allotted time. With learning, don't be afraid to quit while you are ahead. If you try and force yourself to study for longer than what you usually pay attention to, you will slowly be adversely affecting your studying. It will also create resistance to wanting to study again the next time because you are finishing the event in an adverse state.

Furthermore, understand that your brain is a muscle, so when working towards a big game or an academic test, we want to maintain our brain energy. We do not want to exhaust our brains before a test. Overstudying before a test is like doing as many pushups as possible before you try for your max lift in the bench press. If you do that, you will not do well, and your muscles will be exhausted. So, do not do that to your brain. If you do, you will take a test with a tired brain the next day. When you think of it like that, you soon realize how damaging it is to your academics. Plan your studying to be ready to take the test the day before. You should invest your time getting good nutrition, exercising, and sleeping the day before a test.

When you finish studying for that period, give yourself a small reward. When I was working on my master's, when I would get ready for a big test, my reward was to get outside and walk around the house after each study session. The exercise would allow my body to pump more oxygen and nutrients to my brain, allowing for a fuller recovery. The benefits of exercise are that I have a better study session when I return to my studies. I would also give myself a big reward after I passed the test. The reward could be as simple as allowing myself to go for a big hike or eat at my favorite restaurant. Adding these small and big rewards will encourage your brain to want to engage in the task again.

Find or create a study group. Study groups can significantly help with your success and theirs. Meeting up is an excellent opportunity to ask your peers questions you might have missed during the lecture. Also, this allows you to clarify concepts you might struggle with. Your classmates, at times, can be better teachers than the teachers. That is because they currently need help to learn the concept, too. The teacher has already learned the concept, so they might need help remembering what grappling with the new idea is like. Study groups also allow you to practice the problems. Ask a classmate to make a pretend test for you. Often, they will create a test that is tougher than the teachers. Having them create a practice test for you is a great way to get the game ready for the test.

If your school has a help center, use it. I struggled with my writing in college, and at times, I still do. I would go into the writing center every time before I turned in an essay. I must admit it was frustrating when I would spend an hour at the writing center and still get a B- on a paper, but I know the grade would have been lower if I hadn't put that time into it. Again, much like study groups, most of the students helping in the help center understand how to solve the problem. If you want to be great at something, surround yourself with people who are great at that thing. They can give you the professional tips and tricks.

When studying, only practice the things that you don't know. Only practicing the things you struggle with might seem self-evident, but for some reason, many students will study what they already know and skip what they don't know. I think it is human nature to try to do what is easiest, knowing that working on problems you struggle with will require more cognitive energy. The irony is that you should save that brain energy for the concepts you don't understand instead of wasting it on ideas you already comprehend. Also, I think part of the avoidance of working on the challenging work is because people do not like sucking at something. Sadly though, you must suck at something before you will get better at it.

Take notes that you can read. I struggled with this in high school and had to learn the skill in college. I had terrible handwriting for a couple of reasons. First of all, I could not spell well, so I would hide behind my lack of ability to spell with poor handwriting. I also tried to write faster than my brain could keep up with. Sometimes, it was because the teacher delivered instruction more quickly than I could keep up with my writing. Other times, I had yet to devise a short-hand method that I was consistent with. Remember, you do not have to write everything word for word. If it is a mathematical problem, you might need every step, but if you are in a lecture, it might benefit you to write down the concept, not the sentence. Knowing how to take specific notes for different classes is where practice comes into play. If you over-simplify your notes, you might miss out on concepts. That is part of the learning process, learning what you need to do to be successful with the content. When you take notes in class, spend the time after or at the end of school to review your notes. Add anything that you need to be able to remember for a later time. At the end, summarize the notes in your own words. Draw a picture if it can help you remember a concept. Reviewing your notes is a great way to strengthen the neurological pathway you create (a new memory).

Be bold and tell the teacher what you want from the class. If you say to your teachers what you want to accomplish, the teacher will often be more willing to help adapt their class to fit your goal. Teachers will often get excited that you know what you want from the class. You might have a naïve understanding at the time between what you want and what you need, but being able to verbalize it is half the battle. If you have some self-advocacy, teachers will be much more willing to work with you and adjust the class to fit your needs. They will understand your shortcomings more if you are upfront and honest about it. Being deliberate with teachers goes back to the stories I told earlier in the book, where I would talk to the teacher. With music, I told the teacher that I did not want to become great at music, but I did enjoy being around it. Letting my teacher know my goals and aspirations also helped the teacher by letting him know to not expound extra effort into trying to mold me into something that I did not want to be.

I have spent some time making stone tools. One method that takes a ton of effort is peck and grind. You bash a rock into another rock to weaken it and then use another rock to grind the material away. Natives would use this method to create axes, mortar, and pedestals. I share this story because the best way to make a stone axe with this method is to find a stone that already has a close shape. In the horse world, we want to train cow-bred horses to cutting horses. We want to make dogs bred to be bird dogs into bird dogs. As a teacher, we want to help a student accomplish their goals. Your teacher will appreciate knowing what you want to accomplish so they can help you to achieve your goals.

My final suggestion is to see your teacher outside of class time. Show them that you are actively trying to learn the information. If you do this, they will be willing to make things work for you. Don't just go in when you need clarification. Occasionally, go in and ask them to make sure you understand the concept. Show them that you have listened to and synthesized the information into your own words. Not only will this make your teacher proud of you, but it will also help you to be in good graces with your teacher. Putting the extra effort in outside of class will be beneficial when grading your work.

Chapter 15: Some Of My Thoughts

SOME OF MY THOUGHTS

A chapter titled Some of My Thoughts leaves my mind open to wander through the abyss of topics, but I will try my best to stay on task. Pre-warning, this will be a longer chapter. I never claim to be right on some of these topics, but some of my ideas are worth saying. Who knows, they may spark people's ideas that change the world. One of my favorite pastimes is talking with some of my intelligent friends. That doesn't sound good when I say it that way. It is not that some friends are more intelligent than others. I genuinely believe everyone is smart in their own right. Some of my friends are more versed in literature and enjoy discussing the complexities of this world. I have always believed that being street-smart and book-smart is essential. For this chapter, I will discuss some things that might be controversial. The topics might be something I believe, or the ideas might just be a thought to consider.

Bullying versus social correction:

One of the academic debates I enjoy having is the school's idea of the slogan of don't be a bully. Treating people wrongly or being mean is not okay, but there is a healthier approach that might get us further as a society. I believe instead of saying don't be a bully; our efforts would be better spent educating students on what to do if they are being bullied. I say this because there will always be bullies in the workplace, life, and society. We have been saying don't be a bully for many years, and I still see kids being mean to each other and adults being mean to each other. So, saying don't be a bully does nothing to solve the problem. Also, in a weird sense, you are being a bully yourself if you tell a bully to stop being a bully. I know that is hard to swallow at first, but the bully would be better served if we honestly explore their motivation for coercive actions. I will examine the complexities of this issue.

Humans are social creatures. We strive for interactions with other humans, and generally, we enjoy this the most with like-minded humans. Wanting to have positive human interactions forces humans into social groups. Social groups form a standard or code that you must live by to maintain your position in the group. I have read books on imprisoned and drug mafiosos, and they even talk about rules and regulations that you must follow. All groups have rules, and in the group arises a person who has to be the policeman. The police officer ensures that the individuals follow the rules, and if they do not, they apply discipline. If the person does not learn and continues the action, the social police officer will kick them out of the group. Not in all cases, but in some, the social police officer maintains order.

It is interesting to me that all groups form some code of conduct. Why is it essential that a group has a code of conduct? Some speculate that it maintains order in a group. It could help form the identity of the group that individuals can then relate to or identify with. Regardless, groups that work together to solve some of the world's most significant problems, all the way to groups of gangsters, all form a set of rules and a social code that you must live by to continue associating with that group.

There is a good amount of mean behavior from kids trying to elevate their status amongst their peers. It is a harsh reality, but it is a reality. I see it in horse herds, cows, dogs, and in most groups. Everyone fights for position to some degree. Everyone has some idea of what they will allow to happen to them and what they will not allow. However, one contention I hold is that not everyone knows what they will not allow to happen to them, and that is in a dangerous position. I also highly encourage that it should become a top priority to figure out what you are willing to endure if you have not done so already. If you do not know what you will not allow to happen to you, this is how people can be sucked into an abusive relationship or be taken advantage of. That said, mean behavior or peer conflict is different from bullying.

You can observe peer conflict between two friends or even just two associates. The idea of being a bully suggests that one person has the upper hand or that it is not a fair fight. They might have the upper hand because they are physically bigger, have a higher title in the workplace, hold more power, are older, or many other combinations. There is a big difference between a kid being mean to a kid versus being a bully. Also, the act of being a bully has some intention of doing physical or mental harm to an individual. So, if a person in a group assumes the role of the social police officer, they may or may not be acting as a bully. Suppose they are administering punishment for behavior outside the group's social norms with the intent of helping the person to become more socially aware. In that case, this person is not being a bully. They are trying to help, not harm. If they use their power for malicious gain, their actions could be considered bullying. If they intend to hurt or harm the individual, the behavior could be viewed from the bully lens. For that reason, you have to be careful when discerning the intentions of a person's actions.

There are also cases where appearance is abnormal that kids will make fun of. It can be hard to deal with when kids are made fun of because they look different. The reason behind it, biologically speaking, is relatively simple. The group does not want the genetics that caused the abnormality to persist.

During the winter, we take a bus ride through a reservation where a bunch of horses were turned loose back in the economic downfall of 2008. I point these herds out to my assistant coaches and explain that you can tell the older herds that have been established for a more extended period. They all tend to be similar in color. After several years of breeding, the group tends to be normal. By normal, I mean they are all close to the same color and height. For some reason, animals and people will gravitate towards what looks and acts like them in nature and with humans. The example I gave is by no means justifying racism. I am just noticing this biological tendency. I believe this drive to identify with a like group becomes even more vital after maturation. Babies will play with other babies across species, but we tend to see this behavior diminish after maturation.

Why might this be so important for the group? Some theorized that groups want to act and look alike so that if there is a battle, they can quickly identify who is in their tribe.

Now that we have a small understanding of why a group might need to maintain an identity, how can we help students in school with this issue? If we could teach the kids being bullied how to have successful friendships and relationships, they might not get bullied as much. In this case, one must debate which came first, the chicken or the egg. What I mean by this is, did the kid become socially strange because of how their peers treated them, or were they socially deviant and their peers mistreated them for their weird behavior? I often feel that these kids were inadequately socialized as young children. Their parents or parent may need to gain the skills or tools to teach their kids how to have healthy relationships. You can't teach skills that you do not have yourself.

So, how can we teach students to be more socially appropriate? Helping students socially can be a challenging endeavor that many teachers are not qualified to do, but it is pretty simple once you boil it down. Identify what the student is doing to bother their peers. Explain to them what they are doing and how it makes others feel. These are tough pills to deliver and tough pills to swallow. But if students want positive peer relationships, they may try to change. If the change rewards them, there is a chance to progress the individual into having more positive relationships. Sometimes, you have to teach students how to be friendly and respectful to each other. Kids will only want to befriend a pleasant kid.

A proper, honest complement can take you a long way socially. Be present in the conversation by being willing to listen when they talk. Refrain from interrupting when they are talking. Take turns when it comes to sharing. The most challenging thing I work hard on teaching students is when someone is saying something mean. Instead of being mean back, inform them that you do not appreciate what they said or did. If you tell them not to do it again, this typically works. If they are unwilling to respect your request, I will do my best not to associate with them. I tell students that once you verbalize your request, it takes the burden of respect off your shoulders and places the burden of respect onto the other person. The other person then has the opportunity to show you if they are a respectable person or not.

Walking away from those being mean to you makes it hard for them to continue to be mean to you. Learning to walk away from mean behavior can be emotionally complicated because it feels like they won. When done right, you're not engaging with that person because they have yet shown you, they are willing to respect your request. You have so much confidence and self-worth to know that their mean remarks are not worth your emotional energy. It shows a level of maturity that the other person does not have. It is controlling your environment and not letting someone else control your feelings. People will learn from word of mouth that you will not tolerate being disrespected. It can even activate the push-pull effect. If you walk away, it leaves the other person wanting your attention. In later interactions, they are pulled into wanting to gain your approval.

To sum it up, I believe that we have to be careful when we call someone a bully. We must know their true intention before accurately identifying what they are doing. I think that it is essential for a group to maintain some social order. I believe that, as school teachers, our efforts would be better assigned to helping the kid who is being bullied. Teach the student how to deal with mean behavior and be willing to change their behavior if it is not accomplishing what they want. Teaching students what to do socially will achieve so much more for the entire group than just telling kids not to be a bully.

Prejudice versus racism:

The next topic I would like to explore is prejudice. For some reason, this word has a negative connotation, but it is useful socially. Many groups add more to the definition, but I lean towards a simpler idea of what it is. Prejudice is the idea based on your first observation that you place judgment. Those are the key essentials when defining it and the basis I will use for this section. I will boil it down to the most innocent, and then we will tackle the more challenging issues that most do not want to admit or discuss.

In the most innocent manner, if I walk into a room with a fireplace. Let's say I cannot feel the heat, and I cannot see the flame, but I can see the metal glowing red hot. I will make a prejudiced assumption that the stove is hot and that I should not touch it. This assumption may be accurate, but it is a reasonable assumption to keep me safe, given the circumstances. As a horse trainer, I must do this whenever I work with a new horse. I have to decide before I walk into the pen with the horse if it is going to kill me or not. I have to look at the horse, and I have to instantly see if it has the potential to learn or the potential to harm. All of this has to be deduced by observing the horse's behavior and its look. Based on my first observations, I must judge whether this is a safe environment to place myself in. It is important to note that once you have further information if you hold onto your original judgment, it can move from a good thing to a bad one. Once you have this newfound understanding, this is where prejudice can evolve into racism. Thinking thoughts and making assumptions based on visual stimuli are not bad things. If you see a dog baring its teeth, this tells you that you better tread carefully. If you see deep signs of rage on a person's face, you should avoid them. You can judge a book by its cover, but if you hold onto those same assumptions after you read some of it, this is what can lead you down the road from having a healthy prejudice to an unhealthy racism. Maybe the book reads just like you would have guessed by the cover, then by all means, good job for guessing that correctly. Perhaps the book is better or worse than what you thought it would be. At this point, I have to turn to Martin Luther King Jr., "not judged by the color of their skin but by the content of their character." Prejudice should keep you safe and respectful in new social situations. It does not have to be some ignorant thought that everyone prefers a particular thing.

Now, the premise is built to explain the challenging piece. Prejudice tells me when I look at a person of color that saying a racial slur might not be the respectful thing to do. They very well could be a person who does not matter what you say, but they could be the person who decides to beat the living tar out of me for saying something of that nature. It depends on the relationship you build with the person. You can speak the exact phrasing in a respectful manner and also in the meanest manner possible. The example I use on this is the term cowboy. Some people have said, "Wow, that guy is a heck of a cowboy!" That phrase can be a huge compliment when the right person tells you those words. People have also said, "I thought you were just a cowboy." Insinuating that they were surprised that I was not dumb, ignorant, and a disgrace. Do not let your prejudice blind you from seeing the beauty that another human might have to offer, but also, don't be blind to the visual circumstances around you.

So, how can we fix this issue of prejudices growing into racism? I believe that the only way to break down prejudices and not allow them to manifest into racism is by having conversations. We have to be able and feel safe to ask the tough questions. Then, we must listen to what the other person has to say. I was talking to a Native American about his struggles growing up Native. He felt he had to work twice as hard to make something of his life. I then asked him if that was a curse or a blessing because he found a way to work twice as hard as before. We then talked about my struggles growing up white in a reservation town. The mean behavior that I received from Natives because I was different from them, but the blessing was that it taught me who I was. It taught me to define myself instead of letting others define me. We left the conversation understanding that we all have struggles. To say one person's struggle is more challenging than another's diminishes what they went through. Any amount of growth will require some amount of strife. Every person's journey is equally important to them. Only through the conversation can we gain some perspective. We will never truly understand, but we can increase compassion, respect, and empathy for the other person.

To look past a person's exterior and into the depths of who they are can lead to the idea of color blindness. I have heard the argument that you need to see their color to recognize where they came from. But if you pick ten random people of a particular color, they most likely share very little commonality. In the famous words of Dale Brisby, "It's not where I'm from; it's where I am going, and I am going to the next one, ol son!" Your past is important because your past experiences shape who you are today. I recognize that, but just because you did poorly at the last rodeo does not mean we should treat you any differently at the next rodeo. It is not the bad things that shape who you are but how you act in those tough times. You can either use the tough times as motivation to improve or the hardships as an excuse for your lack of character.

Academic Downfalls Due to Race or Poverty:
The real monster to blame is poverty, not color. It does not matter if you are a poor white kid, a poor black kid, a poor Mexican kid, or a poor whatever other kid. You are less likely to rise above poverty. There are many issues at play. One issue that tends to affect children in poverty affects their cognitive function. To be more intelligent, make sure you are getting proper nutrition, sleep, and exercise. Kids growing up in poor areas are likelier not to have those needs met. Their diet tends to be junk food, sugar, and energy drinks. Given these facts, it surprises me that teachers wonder why they cannot pay attention in class. Often, these children do not have the cognitive energy to do anything academically challenging. Many times, drug rates are higher in poor communities. Higher drug rates can lead to many disadvantages, from their sleep being interrupted by mom or dad's drunken stupor to a kid lying awake

at night wondering if their parent is going to be okay. Then, when the kid does make it through the night the following day, they are fed a sugary cereal or donut. The kid has a slight bit of energy from the sugar before they come crashing down.

I have had this argument regarding our English Language Learner students. We have had professionals say we are not meeting our English Language Learners (ELL) students' needs, which is true. After diving deep into our numbers, I realized that some of our top-performing students are ELL students. So, what was the difference? Suppose the ELL student comes from college-educated parents who understand the importance of education. In that case, their parents can afford to feed them good food, and they can participate in sports because they do not have to work to help earn money for the family. ELL students from those families are more likely to get better grades. These ELL students also tend to come from smaller families. A baby crying in the middle of the night can disrupt the other kids' sleep. A tired kid will learn poorly. A malnourished kid will not be able to focus well in class. Finally, a kid who needs proper exercise might be unable to sit still and focus on the class content.

This gal I was discussing this concept with then said, "Wouldn't it be better to focus on something we can change and not something that we cannot change?" Well, yes and no. Putting a cast on an arm when the leg is broken will not help the leg heal. We as educators have to accurately address the problem so that we can have a chance at fixing it. Identifying a problem just because it is politically cool at the time will not help resolve the real issue. It also turned out that once an ELL student rose to a particular academic proficiency level, they were removed from the ELL program. So, this led to only the failures being left in the program. These educational professionals then tried to say that we were not teaching the ELL students adequately. Again, if you did the same thing with the poor white kids, you would see the same evidence of a lack of teaching the poor kids.

Science verse creativity:

Another issue that I have found to be engaging in the scientific community is having one's thoughts and opinions and not being afraid to say them. There will be no new ideas if we accept what science says about everything. Instead, why not question everything in science so it doesn't fail?

One example of questioning science that I find interesting to reflect on is an issue that arises in psychology, and the example goes something like this: 70% of the people performed this way. They may have pushed the button; they may have been the jailors that acted aggressively, or maybe it is some other thing measured. I have always been interested in the null group or why the other group did not do what the normal group did. It might have to do with free will. A gift from God, and once he lives in us, we are no longer tied down to acting like feral beings. For some reason, science has a hard time when you bring God into it.

Religion often has a hard time when you bring science into it. Maybe science and God are more connected than science would like to admit. I was fortunate enough to go to a lecture by Dr. Jason Lisle. He had a great way of melting science and the bible together. Science and religion do not have to fight against each other; on the contrary, if pride is set aside, they can learn from each other.

I am not claiming that I know the answer, but I have always joked that I know the one who knows the answer to all things. The exciting thing is that science needs innovation, the ability to develop a creative idea that is something new. It is the same thing that science tends to shun. I apologize for pointing out the hypocrisy in these systems. It is essential to recognize and change it to improve as a society. We can't fix the bully by bullying them, and we can't shun new ideas in science if we are going to solve problems and develop creative solutions.

Create a routine of occasionally breaking routines:

Another issue I have spent a good bit of time thinking about is what I told my roommate, "Make rules, follow the rules, but don't be afraid to break the rules occasionally." Needing a routine but getting tired of doing the same thing brings out another human hypocrisy I have often considered. As humans, we like a pattern, structure, and routine. Many people will spend a ton of time creating a routine. The routines are good. They help us maximize the little time that we have. The problem with routines is that they are boring, so we have to make a routine to break up our routines and do something that we wouldn't normally do.

Hate speech versus free speech:

Another mainstream idea currently is the idea of hate speech versus mean speech versus free speech. These are tough topics to cover. By no means do I think you should be mean; in the same way, I do not believe in being a bully. I am not even justifying hate speech, but intellectually speaking, we must understand it and its roots. Should someone be able to say something mean to another person? I think they should. You should have the right to hate people, to hate things, and to hate ideas. I encourage people to be respectful in the process, but even that can be a complex concept to understand. One person's idea of being respectful will be different than another person's idea of what being respectful is. In many ways, it is a non-definable, much like love. We can have many good definitions of love, hate, or respect, but it is more of a process than a definition.

I might have someone call me a ginger because I am a redhead. I grew up not liking being called ginger because, in high school, kids would inform me that it was kick and ginger day and would proceed to kick me for no reason. They might call me ginger and legitimately describe me with the only vocabulary they possess. I then have the responsibility to tell them I do not prefer to be called a ginger. I like to be called a redhead, or even better, they can call me by my name. Unless I verbalize that I do not like being called ginger, they do not have the opportunity to be respectful to me. That is where we go so wrong with the idea of hate speech.

I define hate speech only after the counterparty has conveyed or requested not to use that term. As a society, different issues must be discussed in public for others to organize what they believe in. People should be given both sides to the argument, and then they should decide what they believe in. As mature humans, we must remember that ideas are not right or wrong but just ideas. Sometimes, what is right in one situation will not necessarily be correct in another situation. Just because someone does not believe in what we believe does not mean we have the right to be mean to them. You should be thankful that you know where they stand, and then ask yourself if that is a person that you want to associate with. As social humans, we tend to groups of like-minded people. You can follow the norm or challenge yourself if you understand that concept. If you challenge yourself and hang around people who don't necessarily have the same opinions, you can grow your perspective.

I believe in avoiding sugar as much as I possibly can. But it is not my job to tell people that they are wrong for eating sugar. If they ask me about the issue, I can explain my reason for avoiding sugar, but it is their choice what they do with the information. Just because we disagree on this belief doesn't mean that we can't be friends. I never ask my friends to avoid eating sugar in front of me because that is their choice, and this is my choice. I do not ask people to change their menu because of my beliefs. I find what I can eat or starve until I can find something that I can eat. This parallel idea can be expounded into hate speech and any other challenging, controversial topic we might create.

Why we do what we do professionally speaking:

As many different teachers as there are, there are many other ideas on how one might best approach our profession. When teaching, a principal once asked me why I taught the way I taught. I chuckled and responded, "Given all the research I have done, this is the best way to help the greatest number of students." That comment led me into another rabbit hole of thinking. I do not believe we as humans do something to intentionally be wrong or, at least, this is not the expected behavior. A first-year teacher has the same intention as a tenth-year teacher. A first-year teacher might have fewer tools and less understanding than a tenth-year teacher, but they still are trying to do what is best for students, given their knowledge. As a person, you will never know all there is to know about something. You might know more than others, and you might even be top in your field, but you will still never know everything there is to know about a subject. In the science world and at higher levels of academia, you will hear the phrase the more you learn about something, the more you realize how little you know about it. If you act on the premise that every person is trying to do the right thing with the tools that they currently have, we can help add to their toolset.

In all learning and relationships, ask yourself, is this person building me up or trying to cut me down? If they are trying to cut you down, get them out of your life as soon as possible. If you can't teach them how to be respectful to you, then they don't deserve your time. One must also understand and be self-aware enough to see if the advice they give you is a form of healthy pruning or punitive and self-seeking.

Pruning for the betterment of the whole:

I have recently been learning more about gardening from a good friend. She was so kind to give us some of her strawberry plants. We planted them in the bed that we had built. After about a week, they were looking okay, but they were not looking happy. My gardening friend came over and explained that we needed to cut the struggling leaves off the plants. At first, I thought this might kill the plant, but she explained that the plant was sending all its nutrients to try and repair the dying parts of the plant. If we eliminate those parts stealing the nutrients, the plant can use those nutrients to create new healthy parts. Sure enough, after we pruned the nearly dead parts, a week later, the plant was growing fresh, healthy leaves. The plants were back to looking healthy and happy again.

I was reading one of Friedrich Nietzsche's books, *Beyond Good and Evil*, and he brought this idea to my head. He explained that if a group or a society is overly protected and all resources are provided, the group will not fight with each other, but the population can perpetuate abnormalities. They also can become lethargic and complacent. All of these things can be detrimental to the longevity of the species. An example is when a family takes pity on a disfigured or handicapped dog. It would surely die in nature but can live on because humans provide safety and food. If this animal reproduces, it can pass on its genes, like bad hips, to the next generation. If this continues for multiple generations, it can lead to a population that cannot survive independently.

Some governments seek to set up a population in this way. A society dependent on the government creates a necessity for the government, which establishes the government's economic value. In our lives, we must prune away these parts that prevent us from growing to our fullest potential. As a free society, we must not allow parts to become dependent without providing production. Pruning can be a hurtful process. So, as teachers, we must approach that with our students with the utmost respect and care. The same goes for correcting our society. It is a painful process necessary for the betterment of the whole. It is a matter of being encouraged, not enabled. We can currently see this happening in many major cities across our country. Large populations have been enabled instead of encouraged, resulting in a significant economic downfall. Not to mention, it erodes the social structure as well.

Be careful with the messages that you send to kids:

They can read between the lines better than you might think. They can hear your intentions loud and clear. I hear many teachers say, "Yay, it is Friday." This statement is reasonably innocent but can send students the wrong message. When you say this statement to students, you tell them that you do not want to be around them and that working with them is exhausting. It may be accurate, but someone might look fat in that dress, and you do not need to say so. Now you change the exact phrase to I am excited to get some rest this weekend, and you now take the harshness out of the statement. I have heard teachers say so many other statements that are so damaging.

I wish you would act normal. The irony of the statement is the student might be acting the way they normally do, and you are essentially telling the student that their normal is not okay. That means that you are saying that they are not okay. That can be damaging.

You need to try harder. Again, we are trying to be encouraging, but if you find yourself saying that, take a step back and realize that you need to teach better. It would help if you showed the student another way to view it. They may need to hear the same thing multiple times. When we give instructions, they might only comprehend the first part. They then practice that part, and their brain is ready to understand the next part of the instructions. That is part of the learning process that should be encouraged, not discouraged.

Students often form these ideas and notions about themselves as students because of the messages their teachers send them. They think and will say that they are dumb or stupid. They will feel that they are not good at math. They will assign themselves these degrading names because they take more time to learn something than their peers. Keep your talk encouraging. Show them the positive side of things. Tell them what they can do, not what they can't do. Finally, be patient with them. If you don't know what to say, ask them a question for further understanding. If you have no advice, which is better, ask them what they can do to help themselves. If you have to give your students advice, provide them with a couple of options and have them pick what they think will be best.

Improvement verse coercion:

I sometimes struggle with how many principals approach academics by encouraging teachers to do more for less by saying, "Well, don't you want to improve your teaching?" I understand the idea of a growth mindset. When I heard this statement, I thought to myself, so what you're saying is that my teaching is not good enough.

Why is it wrong to get to the professional level and want to maintain that level? You might still improve, but you will notice only a slight change in things. In five years of learning a sport, your ability and growth in a sport is enormous. You are learning the rules, you learn techniques, and you learn strategy. When you become a professional, the adjustments might mean a lot in the fine details of the sport but will mostly go unnoticed. When I work on riding a horse, I build my cues down to inches and fractions of inches. Many riders cannot notice the change in my cue that allows the horse to go from a circle to a lateral to a lead. I will always work on improving my teaching. Trying to motivate teachers with that statement is not recognizing the time and effort they put in to get where they are.

If that statement comes from somebody who is not as good of a teacher as I am, I sometimes can't help but chuckle. It would be like a middle school baseball player telling King Griffey Jr. what he needs to do to improve his swing. The kid might be correct, and Griffey will be smart enough to recognize the truth when presented to him. But, most of the time, the kid's instruction will be basic in understanding when Griffey is working on small details that the kid cannot even comprehend.

Motivation versus Intimidation:

A final thought I would like to explore in this chapter is the idea of motivation. I will start with a couple of questions. What motivates students to learn? What motivates students to try their best? What motivates you to put your best work forward? Do you always put your best foot forward at your job? What inspires your kids to do things that they don't want to? Is one motivation better than another kind of motivation? Have what motivated students changed over the last ten, fifteen, or twenty years? From what I have observed, motivations change with time. I hate to over-simplify it down to this analogy, but motivations are trends much like clothing is to style. In the same sense that not everyone has the same style, not everyone will be motivated by the same things. Since kids picked on me a bunch in school, my motivation at that time was to prove them wrong. I wanted to grow up to be somebody and show them that the little kid that they made fun of was way more than just an object of harassment.

I think back to the people that have motivated me in my life. What qualities did they possess? Was this something I could learn or some God-given talent? Many of the people who inspired me in my life are people that I looked up to. These leaders have passed the silent test of hypocrisy. What they suggested to me was a quality that they had mastered themselves. They didn't try and control me. They had my best interest in mind. They didn't try to lump me into some big category that was a minuscule aspect of my life, like my age, hair color, or the fact that I am a cowboy.

My dad was explaining to me a gentleman that he admired and someone that motivated him. One of the things that my dad respected about the gentleman was he never told my dad what to do. He listened to what my dad had to say and showed my dad the choices he had at hand. He would have my dad decide what would work best for him. He then had him report back after my dad had implemented his choice. Advising my dad in this method was a strong motivation to help empower him to be in control of his life. Instead of giving my dad the answer, he forced him to find his answer. He encouraged him to solve his problems instead of intimidating my dad to do what he thought was best. Then, he encouraged my dad to reflect and ask himself if his choice helped him get what he wanted. We cannot be afraid of making mistakes, but if we mess things up, adjust and try something new.

I have read several books on this topic, and they also explore the changing motivation in society. One of the books I read on motivation was *Creating Innovators* by Tony Wagner. The book explains how the new generation gravitates towards jobs they believe will help change the world. Each generation changes what influences and inspires them. In a societal way, it follows Maslow's Hierarchy of Needs. A certain level of needs must be met for the society to advance to the next stage. If a society struggles with providing adequate food for all its members, it won't be able to contemplate issues of morality or intellectual ideas. Interestingly, each generation claims to be more morally correct than the prior generation. I don't think this concept will change. Adults will think kids are messing things up, and they will continue to believe that adults don't understand what they are going through because it has to be vastly different than when their parent was a kid.

Looking back in history, we can see, on average, a change in what working people are willing to do. Not too far in America's history, many southern states were still getting away with the idea of the company line. A company could move into a small rural community and provide housing and goods in trade for work in sub-human conditions. That is looking at that situation through the dangerous lens of ethnocentricity. At the time, working for the company was a better option than other living conditions, so people chose to work for the company. Even though every year, they got deeper into debt. But they had more than if they were trying to farm a small plot of land. Their kids had at least an opportunity to be educated and socialized with other kids their age.

So, what motivates people? There is this deep-down desire to provide something better for one's offspring. Immigrants often come to this country of America and work strenuous jobs. Why? Because honestly, the hard job they are working here in America is better than the hard job they would be working in Mexico (or another country). Immigrants are getting paid more to perform their jobs, and they can provide a better life for their kids.

Trying to provide better for one's kids often leads parents into this paradox that is approached with a purist heart but is implemented incorrectly. Good kids are ruined because their parents make their life too easy. Often, I see parents work so hard to provide their kids with everything instead of teaching them how to acquire what they desire. As the old sang goes, feed a man a fish, and he will go hungry tomorrow. Teach a man to fish, and he will hunger no more. If implemented in the wrong way, it leads to entitlement. Kids think they deserve all these things without working for them. That is a dangerous position that leads a society to entitlement. We are currently seeing many of the repercussions of this.

As I circle back, this is where we see motivations change from one generation to the next. It used to be admirable to work a job to provide for your family. Then it shifted into this idea of working a job because you enjoy it. Some scholars argue that now, a motivation for this next generation is seeking employment that benefits the world and is also something they enjoy doing. Overall, the more you can diminish yourself and seek this bigger than yourself, the deeper your maturity is. The ultimate end means to this is sacrificing yourself for the betterment of society. Self-sacrifice is why figures like Martin Luther King Jr., Mohammad Gandhi, and Jesus were such influential figures. They gave their self for this greater good!

So, what motivates you? Greatness motivates. Selflessness motivates. Leaders motivate. Authentic relationships with other people can motivate. This idea of a better future motivates people. Call it greedy, but this idea of wanting more easily inspires ingenuity. Creating something new motivates. Creating something better motivates. Some people are striving to make more money so you can spend more time doing what you enjoy. But also, fun motivates, comedy motivates, music motivates, and art motivates people to feel. Teachers say students are immune to feelings because they are bombarded with inspirational stuff on social media. The students are overloaded with content to the point that the message is no longer touching. What motivates kids today will not necessarily motivate students tomorrow. I often tell teachers a reward is only a reward if it is something students want. Rewards and punishments only motivate students if they encourage a deeper level of action. If not, then the motivational means are broken or no longer effective.

Chapter 16: What Is Important

WHAT IS IMPORTANT

What is important is a question that many people have explored. With that question being such a big topic, it can be daunting even to develop a tool to measure what is important. You can interview a thousand different people, and though they might have similar answers, the differences will be just as complex as the number of people you interviewed. Is the question worth exploring, or will pursuing that question create more problems? I have recently been thinking about this question and decided it might be the best way to finish this book aside from the Mr. B'isms.

This winter, while writing this book, my Grandma passed away. A combination of several different cancers, including three tumors in her brain that were rapidly growing, is what put an end to the beautiful life that she lived here on this earth. In the end, Grandma went pretty fast. Thanksgiving, she felt a bit tired. In December, Grandma tripped and fell a couple of times. By the end of December, she didn't recognize the house she was in except for her bedroom. During the final week, getting her out of bed was hard.

As a family, it was a hard place to be. We all knew the end was coming fast, so we wanted to spend every second with her. But, if she was sleeping and heard her great-granddaughters, she wanted nothing more than to be around them. Is this idea of family the most important thing?

Many people contest the importance of family. Generally speaking, most animals have some intrinsic motivation to procreate. If reproducing is the most important thing, then how would parents ever be able to be mean to their kids? How could abuse be prevalent? How would fathers or mothers be able to walk away from their kids?

I had a friend in High school. Her mom had her when she was 16. She grew up poor and in government support. Then, a stepdad came into the picture. I remember my friend telling me how excited she was to have him in her life because that meant they could finally afford crayons for school.

Sadly, the stepdad started touching her inappropriately. When she was old enough to understand that how the stepdad touched her was not okay, she told her mom. That started the cycle that made her life a living hell. The stepdad accused her of lying and proceeded to convince her mother that she was a problem child. When my friend was in her teens, the way her mother and stepdad treated her was beyond emotionally abusive. My friend was physically abused by her stepdad as well. It got so bad my friend tried to use drugs to escape the pain, and when drugs were not strong enough to escape reality, she tried committing suicide.

What would cause a parent to completely turn on one of their kids and put them through trauma so strong that their kid felt their only way out was to end their life? Maybe it was just the perception of a teenage youth struggling to understand life. It was not until after my friend cut all ties with her family that she was able to start to heal.

I know this is not the only case where our own family has been the most abusive people in our lives. I have seen students come through my classroom where I was hoping and praying that they would make it to 18 so they could get out on their own. So why is family so important to some and the creation of hell on earth for others? Is there something more important than family? How can we live in a family where the members thrive and grow instead of being defeated and oppressed?

The Bible says that when husband and wife come together, they must leave their parents and cleave to each other. They are still a part of each other's family but also a new entity. With Cain and Abel, their fight was not with some other person but within the family. Joseph's brothers sold him into slavery because of the jealousy that ended up ripping that family apart. There is story after story about the cruelty families can impose on each other, not just in the Bible but also in modern-day life.

What is more important than family? I will argue that it is God. Being a Christian, the one that has created all existence deserves to be the most important thing. Living a life in him is how we can better understand what is important to him and what should be essential to us. The New Testament says that the most important commandment is to love your God with all your heart, and the second is to love your brother as yourself. Once we dive further into this, we can find and see the most important thing. Below God himself, the next most important thing in our existence is love. What is love, how does it act, where do we find love, and can we improve it?

I believe that many Christians fall prey to being judgmental because they focus more on the other commandments, what I might call tangible commandments. When it says thou shall not murder, you can easily count the number of people you have murdered. You can quantify that commandment. The quantifiableness makes a person judgmental because they can say, "I am such a good Christian because I have not done this or because I read my bible every day." It gets tricky when you ask them how much love you have shown today. Answering the question is challenging because love is immeasurable. You can't say, "I have shown ten pounds of love today!"

Webster defines love, and I invite you to look that up. The Bible even offers some level of its definition of love in 1 Corinthians 13. Also, as the Bible says, "And now these three remain: faith, hope and love. But the greatest of these is love." If love is one of the greatest things to God, why would he make it such a challenging concept to grasp and understand fully? My belief is when love gets confusing, he wants us to talk to him about it. It is our Father in Heaven's way of making a relationship essential. He delights in that, and in turning to him, he shows us more and more of what love truly is. The Lord does not give us all the answers because he wants us to ask him the question and consciously obey what he has to offer us.

I was having an excellent discussion about this concept with a great friend. We can only love as much as we know of love. I will admit the caveat that some people try to love others more than they love themselves. But they know that level of love. Unfortunately, they do not administer that level of love to themselves. Where do we learn love from? Parents, family, friends, people in our lives, mentors, and most perfectly God.

Why is it that family can devour individuals? It is because there is a lack of love. I tell my students you are either part of the problem or a part of the solution, and there is no middle ground. To some degree, love falls into the same water as that analogy. Either you are actively pursuing love, or you're not. I defined love to my buddy when he asked me to explain it in as few words as possible as wanting what is best for someone else. When we have a relationship with another person, are we genuinely a loving friend if we always agree with them and never challenge them? Most people do not want that in a friend. What if we continuously tell them how they are doing everything wrong and the right way they could do it? This contentious friend is not what we want and is not a loving relationship. The Bible says that the Lord is the perfect balance between truth and love. The balance of truth and love is what we must aspire to. The interesting word in that sentence is balance. Balance is interesting because you realize that a different proportion of love and truth must be administered in each situation. One person might only handle 1 pound of truth to 10 pounds of love, whereas the next person might need 10 pounds of truth to 1 pound of love. The balance may change depending on the person and where they might be developmentally.

Love is why a friend can be more important than a family member. Do we not prioritize our time with the people we believe love us the most? As I sit and write those words, the thing that jumps out to me is knowing that God loves us the most, but many of us do not prioritize God in our lives. Even though we do not prioritize God, he is our most significant source for learning about love. I do not think he would want us to completely isolate ourselves from everything else and only sing him praise. We will have plenty of time for that when we are in heaven. When I mentor a student, whether in academics or with training horses, I have always said I must teach them a concept and work with them on it. Then, I must leave and allow them to explore the idea independently. You can be best friends with someone, but you will need a break from them at some point. In parallel with that concept, the Lord wants us to invest our time in him and learn more about his love. Then, we must go into the world and show others the love we have learned from him.

One of my contentions is that our understanding of love only grows when we invest our time in God. Someone might debate this and then ask how can an un-Godly person learn about love then? Well, simply put, just because they do not believe in God does not mean that they are immune to the effects of him. For example, someone could believe the sun does not cause skin cancer. Just because they think that the sun does not cause cancer does not mean that they are immune from getting skin cancer. Simply put, your beliefs do not dictate what the actual truth is.

Still, how does a non-believer learn about love? Is it that they are learning about it in a second-hand form? Similarly, a person can hear their friends talk about a book that their friends have read, so they can have a conversation about the book from what they have seen and heard from their friends. But they have yet to read the book themselves. This example is more prevalent in today's day and age, with the ease with which we can access information. Many people in academia will talk about an author, a quote, or something they have watched on YouTube. They need to read the actual writing in its totality to understand the author's intention. So, an un-godly person learns about God's love from others, a second-hand source. They know love but can never wholly understand it unless it is in God himself. I do not believe we can ever truly understand God's love during our lives. We are merely like a graph approaching its asymptote. We get closer to God's love the further we pursue it, but our earthly minds will never understand a concept as complex as God's love.

Also, understand what makes this example even more complex is this idea; if we had ten different people write down their interpretation of a fine piece of art, we very well could get ten completely different responses. Here is where the third piece of my argument comes into play. The interpretation of the fine art piece comes from the person's relationship with the art. I am not being wildly absurd in my understanding that you cannot have an actual relationship with an art piece, but, in a sense, you can. Based off of your previous experiences is what will shape your interpretations. Based on your perspective on the art piece, whether you're a long distance away, close up, standing to the left, or know the artist, your interpretation of the art will depend on all these factors. We see this to be true with relationships with people as well. How often have you discovered that they tore down your initial perception of them after you got to know somebody? Also, the personal feelings you are engrossed in can shape your interpretation of the art in the same way that they might affect your relationship with a person. If you are sad and depressed, this will change how you receive art and how you act in a relationship.

The third most important thing I would like to explore is the idea of a relationship. All humans and animals have this desire for a relationship. In relationships, this is where we can foster love. The Bible, even with the most important commandments, encourages the idea that we must have a relationship with our God and with other people. You cannot love your brother as thy self if you do not have some relationship with your brother.

We also see relationships between animals, which points to the idea that relationships are part of all animals' basic needs. When I was in middle school, I had a beautiful Australian Shepherd. She was a red mural with a half-blue eye. I called her Bobby because she had four little white bobby socks for her feet. I trained her to do all kinds of tricks from the usual, like sitting, lying down, shaking, and rolling over. I also taught her some unusual tricks like playing dead, praying, ringing the bell to go outside, crawling, spinning around, turning off lights (Grandpa's favorite), picking up pine cones for him, and yes, even later in my years when I was old enough, to get a beer out of the fridge. I have to admit teaching her to get a beer out of the refrigerator had nothing to do with drinking beer because, at the time, I didn't. But my roommate said it would be cool if I could teach my dog that. So, I had to show him that I could.

Anyway, that dog had a friend she would play with, and her name was Brooke; she was a black retriever. They had the most fun playing together. I joked Bobby's smile got even more prominent when I told her she would get to play with Brooke. I may have self-imposed this idea of a relationship being there, but I believe it to be true.

I have seen many other relationships with animals, from my horses with other horses to different breeds of animals becoming friends. We acquired a horse at the Christian horse camp. The owner told us that the horse had lost its pasture mate and had been mourning ever since. Their hope was with us having so many horses, maybe this horse could find a new friend. Believe it or not, it did! That Appaloosa horse ended up becoming friends with one of our Tennessee Walkers. In the pasture, you could always find them together. Regardless, even with animals, you can see this need for a relationship with another animal.

We can see this with people with disabilities. It can have remarkable healing effects if we can help them build a relationship with an animal. With people with Post-Traumatic Stress Disorder PTSD, having a companion dog can help them deal with the emotional stress and flooding that they might experience. Kids with social and emotional issues can receive great therapy by spending time with or riding a horse. It can even help the elderly by bringing these service animals around. Regardless, time after time, we can see the importance of the relationships that we have in our lives.

In many ways, if people do not have support at home, these other relationships that they foster can easily be more important than the family they do have. I had another buddy pass away recently. He had a brother, and his parents are still alive. He chose to leave a majority of his things to a friend he had. He decided his constructed relationship with a friend was more important than his blood relation with his brother. His example reminds us how important people can become to us even if they are not blood family. It was because of the relationship these two individuals had fostered with each other that created a deeper-than-family relationship.

I know many times when I was going through family struggles, it would be a friend that I would call and see what they had to say. If you have a healthy family, relationships are still just as significant. If you have little or no family, I still contend that relationships are meaningful, and the desire is still there.

Another example I would like to bring back from my former writing is the idea of the student being bullied. If we can teach them pro-social skills and help them obtain a relationship, we can help them develop the tools to cope with what they are experiencing. All people, and even more so kids, have this need for healthy relationships.

Even more profound on the human side of things, we need relationships because we need to talk to people. Sometimes, we have to say what is on our mind. In doing so, this can help us solve our problems. In other cases, we might need to ask for advice. On another level, we might need to hear a joke or tell one to experience the ecstasy of laughing. If you don't believe me, try this little experiment at home sometime. Tell your favorite joke out loud when there is nobody around. It might be sad how not funny it is, but merely having a person there to respond or not can bring the humor right back to the same joke!

In some of the best relationships, you can be in the person's presence, and things improve. People often say that food tastes better when they are in love. Smells smell better, and time seems to slip away when you are with the person you have created a strong relation-ship with.

One of the humans' worst states of being is boredom. When time seems to slow down to the point where eternity appears to rest in each second, it is tor-ture. It is interesting to me how kids nowadays are so afraid of boredom. This new generation has some form of superficial entertainment right at their fingertips, and the need to be entertained almost drips through their veins like a drug.

The mere fact of having a person there can give a person confidence to do things that they thought they could never do. My Fiancé (now wife) is afraid of heights, and late this winter, we went on a hike that fol-lowed a ridge line. She often said she needed to stop be-cause she was too afraid to keep going. With my friend's encouragement, my Fiancé continued forward. She later admitted that she would have never accomplished that hike if we had not been there to push her.

A converse to this story of how meaningful re-lationships can be is when we see the absence of. One of our nation's most significant punishments is solitary confinement. The removal of all relationships can be harsh on people. It can drive them to levels of insanity. People have reported it as one of the worst things they have ever experienced. People have reported back to my earlier comment that it felt like time was no longer moving. They were stuck in hell on earth, with no end in sight. A life without a relationship almost takes the living part of life out. If we do not have someone to share what is happening to us, we cannot quantify life itself.

Dick Proenneke, if you watch his documentary of him up in the woods, he was extremely isolated. Even with the extreme isolation, he had a bush pilot who would bring him supplies, and he had relationships with little birdies that he had trained to eat out of his hand. As isolated as he was, he still found a way to foster some relationships. His example again points to my fact of how essential relationships are.

There is also this idea of being a lone wolf. Again, there is strength in being able to go off and be alone. It takes a level of self-confidence to allow yourself to be consumed in your thoughts. I argue that even the lone wolf desires relationships. Even if the relationship is used just for procreation, it is still vital to the lone wolf's survival. More commonly, these solitary wolf figures go away from people for extended periods but then come back to the relationships that they have. Most people with this lone-wolf mentality have relationships but keep very few friends. These lone wolf people have a tight inner circle. They might never be present in the public's eye with these relationships, but they have them nonetheless. I have a friend at school who considers himself a lone wolf. He does not fit in with most of the staff, but he still has a strong relationship with his kids, his parents, and a select few that he lets into his inner circle. Even lone wolves need to revisit their pack occasionally.

When I think back to the several losses I have had to mourn this winter, I can't help but think of the relationship I had with the person. I loved my Grandma, and she loved me. We could talk and confide in each other. She could teach me, and I often taught her as well. Sometimes, she would be a listening ear. Other times, she would try her best to convince me not to do the dumb idea I might have had. When we have family rooted in relationships, God, and love, we can have some of the strongest bonds that could ever exist.

If you want to foster better relationships with people, try loving them more! If you are unsure where to start with love, I recommend you start with the Bible, and 1 Corinthians 13 will help you with that. There is an extensive list of what love is and is not. It can be daunting if your life needs more of what it addresses. If you are struggling with what to do next, pick one of the pieces from Corinthians and show someone one of those aspects. Try the next one once you have become proficient at one part.

If you are to the point where you feel like you have no one else to talk to, try building a relationship with God. Try talking to him. If you have no one else to listen to you, try saying it to him. I have given this challenge to several of my non-believing friends, and they were beyond surprised at how much it helped them. God helped them to the point where they later became believers. The Lord will talk back to you if you slow down and listen to what he says. Start by trying to sit down for ten minutes. Spend as much time as you need to tell him everything in your heart. The rest of the time, be still and be willing to listen. Make sure you have no distractions and are in a comfortable place to focus. He will talk to you if you give him the time and listen. Sometimes, it might be a thought he puts in your head. He sometimes spoke to me through song lyrics or words from a book. Other times, his words have come from my friend's mouth. If you seek his words, he will show you his desires. Understand, sometimes he answers right away, and other times he needs to show you something more so you can understand what he says.

Writing this book has been an incredible journey. It has been fun remembering the different stories and trying my best to put them into words. I hope I depicted the stories how we often tell them while standing around a campfire or sitting around a table enjoying each other's company. Understand that some of these thoughts I might believe, and some of these thoughts might have already changed. Some of these ideas are built on different levels of research, and other ideas come from anecdotal evidence. Some of my thoughts could be to start a conversation or to look at something in a different light.

I believe you should not be afraid to believe what you think and be willing to say what you believe. I believe there is not as much hate in this world as what some news programs and people try to portray. I believe the only way to realize these things is by having tough conversations and asking people what they believe. I believe in listening to people when they talk and listening for understanding. I believe in spreading as much love as one can. I believe the more love we spread, the better this world will get. I believe in change. If you do not like something about yourself, you can change it through hard work. I believe in family and relationships. I believe in education and learning as much as possible. I believe you should constantly be striving to improve yourself in some way. I believe in helping others to learn how to find the fullest potential that they have in themselves. I believe in friendships. I believe in relishing the little moments because, in the end, those can be some of the most important memories. I believe in the connections between learning, training horses, and teaching. Most importantly, I believe in God.

Thank you for your time in reading this book, and I hope these words made you think of these topics differently. I hope these words have helped you learn something you didn't know. I hope these words might have inspired you to improve your life. If so, the time spent writing this book was worth it. Happy trails, and may God bless you!

Chapter 17: Mr. B'isms

MR. B'ISMS

- Common sense ain't cheap these days.
- Don't work for free.
- When you're fighting a fire, it doesn't matter what color socks you have on.
- If it feels like you are making it way harder than it needs to be, you probably are.
- If you do it like everyone else, you will never be better than them.
- If you keep doing what you have always done, you will keep getting what you have always gotten.
- A wise squirrel doesn't put all his nuts in one place.
- In my pursuit of perfection, I have realized that I am not.
- Teach them what they can do, not what they can't do. That is how you build confidence in horses and people.
- After two degrees, I realized that I am an educated idiot.
- Sometimes, it is not even worth being right.

- You can lead a bull by the whiskers to town as long as you stay one step in front of him.
- Monsters are not that scary. They tend to just be your little brother once you pull the sheet off their head.
- If everyone is being mean to you, maybe you are mean to others.
- What you choose to look at is what you will see.
- How much joy and happiness do you add to your life and others daily?
- If a kid gets an F in your class, you have failed that student. Literally, you have failed to teach that student.
- Teach every student how to succeed in your class, and you will be the teacher they need you to be.
- Make the wrong thing hard and the right thing easy!
- When you are teaching, it is not about you. It is about the student.
- You can win a kid over with love!
- Our job is not just to teach good students but to teach all students! Which includes the tough ones.
- The more you try to control kids, the less control you will have over them. The less you try to control students, the more control you will have over them. This is the same with horses.
- It is not how you write it but what you have to say.
- Great literature evokes feelings! Sometimes you agree or disagree, but it should always make you think.
- I love dull days. That means you did the job right!

- One's daily objective should be to try and minimize the number of dumb things that one might do.
- Not belittling the hardships you have endured, but you have to understand that there are far lesser people than you who have endured far more than you have to lay the foundations for your existence.
- Love is desiring the best for someone, even when sacrificing their momentary needs.
- A wolf with its leg caught in a trap can be a dangerous animal, even when you're trying to help it.
- If we only knew the number of lives of people that we have touched without even knowing it!
- You can lead a horse to water, but you can't make them drink. But you can kick them in the butt hard enough to get them wet!
- Hell is hell; which one weighs more, yours or mine? There is no way to measure it.
- Don't argue with another person to try and convince them. Argue to try to state your point in the most precise way possible. Try to define your truth in the best words.
- Give more than you take, but never be afraid to ask for help.
- In the toughest of times, seek knowledge.
- Don't be afraid to change because it will happen whether you like it or not.
- What is true today might not be true tomorrow. That is why the pursuit of truth has to be continuous.
- Infinity can only exist if time exists.

- Love can be found everywhere if you are willing to look for it.
- It is okay to say no.
- Stand up for your beliefs, and don't be afraid to say them.
- Sometimes, crazy ideas might be the best idea.
- Treat your students how you would want to be treated.
- Teach them (horses and students) first before you demand them to do it.
- As a teacher, students look up to you. Are you going to be an excellent example of what to be?
- It is always better to have too many manners than too little. It is always better to be overdressed than underdressed.
- When learning about a concept or ideology, give ample time and energy to both sides before you form your opinion.
- Science has been wrong many times, but God has never been wrong.
- You can strengthen your brain only through hard work, effort, and time.
- Don't get bucked off before you get on the horse.
- Sometimes, a righteous endeavor can lead you into the depths of hell.
- You can accomplish more with a good question rather than telling someone what to do.

CHAPTER 18

Bibliography

- Foer, Joshua. *Moonwalking with Einstein: The Art and Science of Remembering Everything*. Penguin Books, 2011.
- Frankl, Viktor E., et al. *Man's Search for Meaning*. Beacon Press, 2006.
- Maravelas, Anna. *Creating a Drama-Free Workplace: Crucial Strategies for Managing Conflict, Incivility, and Mistrust*. Career Press, 2020.
- Medina, John. *Brain Rules: 12 Principles for Surviving and Thriving at Work, Home and School*. Pear Press, 2014.
- Nietzsche, Friedrich Wilhelm, and Redaktion Gröls-Verlag. *Beyond Good and Evil*. Gröls Verlag, 2023.
- Oakley, Barbara. *A Mind for Numbers How to Excel at Math and Science (Even If You Flunked Algebra)*. TarcherPerigee, 2014.
- Wagner, Tony. *Creating Innovators: The Making of Young People Who Will Change the World*. Scribner, 2012.

CHAPTER 19

Recommended Books

- *12 Rules for Life* By: Jordan Peterson
- *A Cowboy Never Lies: 1 and 2* By: Dan Burnett
- *A Mind for Numbers* By: Barbara Oakley
- *Ben Snipes Northwest Cattle King* By: Roscoe Sheller
- *Beyond Good and Evil* By: Friedrch Nietzsche
- *Bob Fudge Texas Trail Driver* By: Jim Russell
- *Brain Rules* By: John Medina
- *Creating a Drama-Free Workplace* By: Anna Maravelas
- *Epic Survival* By: Matt Graham and Josh Young
- *Evidence-Based Horsemanship* By: Dr. Stephen Peters and Martin Black
- *It Didn't Start with You* By: Mark Wolynn
- *KA-MI-AKIN* By: A.J. Splawn
- *Lost at School* By: Ross W. Greene
- *Mere Christianity* By: C.S. Lewis
- *Moonwalking with Einstein* By: Joshua Foer
- *Power* By: Robert Greene
- *The Black Hand* By: Chris Blatchford
- *Teach Like a Pirate* By: Dave Burgess

- *The Last Cowboys* By: John Branch
- *The power of Different* By: Gail Saltz
- *The Road Back to You* By: Ian Morgan Cron
- *The Shack* By: WM. Paul Young
- *The Way of the Shepherd* By: Kevin Leman and Bill Pentak
- *Trail Dust and Saddle Leather* By: Jo Mora
- *UDL* By: Katie Novak
- *Unoffendable* By: Brant Hansen
- *Willful Blindness* By: Margaret Heffernan